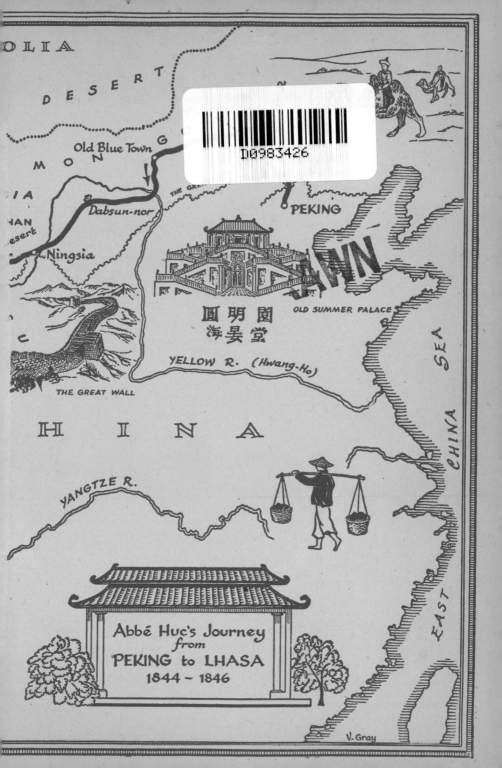

Abbé Huc's Journey *from* PEKING to LHASA 1844 – 1846

HIGH ROAD IN TARTARY

HIGH ROAD
IN
TARTARY

AN ABRIDGED REVISION
OF
ABBÉ HUC'S TRAVELS IN
TARTARY, TIBET AND CHINA
DURING THE YEARS 1844–5–6

EDITED BY
JULIE BEDIER

Illustrated by
JOSEPH NOTARPOLE

New York
CHARLES SCRIBNER'S SONS
1948

EDITOR'S NOTE

The unabridged edition of Abbé Huc's *Travels in Tartary, Tibet and China,* as originally translated from the French by William Hazlitt and published in 1851, is a fascinating study not only of the good Abbé's journey and of the people he met, but of the terrain, the fauna and the flora along the way. Much of the scientific material has been eliminated in an endeavor to present the Abbé's journey as a story, and to bring it out as the mighty tale that it is. After a thorough check with modern Rand McNally's and The National Geographic Society's maps, the remarkable French spellings of Oriental place names were changed to more modern and accepted forms. In some cases, where the places mentioned were too small to appear on any map, Pelliot's spelling was used. For those interested in a complete and annotated edition of this celebrated work, attention is called to that of J. M. Planchet, C.M., *Souvenirs of a Journey through Tartary, Tibet, and China during the Years 1844, 1845 and 1846,* two volumes, Lazarist Press, Peking, 1931.

A WORD

"If the doctrine which these men hold is a false doctrine, the Tibetans will not embrace it. If, on the contrary, it is true, what have we to fear? How can the truth be prejudicial to men?" So spoke the Regent of Tibet about the teaching of the two Catholic priests who had arrived at the forbidden city of Lhasa on January 29, 1846.

Fathers Gabet and Huc, French priests of the Vincentian Order, had made the long and toilsome journey into Tibet from their Chinese mission near Peking. They had crossed arid deserts and frightful mountains, suffering the fatigues of primitive travel and the dangers of hunger, thirst, sickness, raging rivers and freezing storms, savage brigands and wild beasts. If not the first Europeans to penetrate this remote district behind its forbidding mountains, Fathers Huc and Gabet were certainly the first to give us a satisfying account of the country and its people.

Today we have numbers of books, fanciful and otherwise, about Tibet. There are occasional hardy explorers who make the toilsome journey, and of late years the airplane has made communication less difficult. To one who is acquainted with the travels of the two French priests, how charmingly reminiscent are these modern accounts! How little the Tibetans have changed! And those friendly Tartars are still such delightful people! Good old Father Huc, could he return, would know and love them every one.

No book of wild fantasies, Father Huc's story rings true in every detail. Even did not modern travelers corroborate his words, we know instinctively that here is a man who has seen things with his own eyes. He has walked those tortuous paths, and climbed those painful ways; he has examined that strange vegetation, felt those biting winds, talked in friendly fashion with those simple people. Here is no spinner of tall tales, but a sober, observant man who went far and suffered much for the souls of his fellow men. And may the day come soon, that day for which he prayed and labored! A people who are not afraid of Truth ought not to be far from the Kingdom of God.

JULIE BEDIER

Contents

CONTENTS

HIGH ROAD IN TARTARY

1

Frenchmen into Tartars

IN the year 1844 there came to us—Fathers Gabet and Huc, French missioners living in the Twin Ravines section not far from Peking—a message that sent us into the extremes of happiness. For some years, while attending to our flock of Chinese Christians, we had cast longing eyes upon the great stretches of Mongolia and had busied ourselves between whiles in acquiring the Tartar dialects. And now, from the Vicar Apostolic, came instructions for an extended voyage we were to undertake for the purpose of studying the character and manners of the Tartars.

Previous to our departure we had to perform an operation of considerable importance—no other than an entire change of costume, a complete metamorphosis. For we had resolved to adopt the secular dress of the Tibetan lamas. One touch of a razor sufficed to sever the long tail of hair which, to conform with Chinese fashions, we each had so carefully cultivated ever since our departure from France. We put on long yellow robes, fastened at the right side with five gilt buttons and around the waist by a long red sash. Over the yellow robe was a red jacket, with a collar of purple velvet; and a yellow cap, surmounted by a red tuft, completed the new costume.

When everything was ready, we mounted our respective animals and proceeded before daylight on the road to Dolon-nor (Seven Lakes). We were resolved to lay aside

our accustomed usages and to become regular Tartars, but
the progress of our little caravan was not at first wholly successful. We were novices in the art of saddling and girthing
camels, so that every five minutes we had to halt, either to
rearrange some cord or piece of wood that hurt and irritated
the camels, or to consolidate upon their backs, as well as we
could, the ill-packed baggage that threatened, ever and
anon, to fall to the ground.

We advanced, indeed, despite all these delays, but still
very slowly. After journeying about thirty-five li, we quitted
the cultivated district and entered upon the Land of Grass.
There we got on much better; the camels were more at their
ease in the desert, and their pace became more rapid.

Samdadchiemba, our camel driver, was our only traveling
companion. This young man was neither Chinese, nor Tartar, nor Tibetan. Yet, at the first glance, it was easy to recognize in him the features characterizing that which naturalists call the Mongol race. A great flat nose, insolently turned
up; a large mouth, slit in a perfectly straight line, with thick,
projecting lips; a deep bronze complexion—all contributed
to give to his physiognomy a wild and scornful aspect. His
little eyes seemed starting out of his head from under their
lids, wholly destitute of eyelashes. When he looked at a
person, he wrinkled his brow, and he inspired the beholder
at once with feelings of dread and yet of confidence.

Samdadchiemba was a Dchiahour—an ex-lama of a lamasery belonging to the country of that name. At the age of
eleven, he had escaped from his lamasery, in order to avoid
the too-frequent and too-severe corrections of the master
under whom he was placed. He afterwards passed the greater
portion of his youth in vagabondage, sometimes in Chinese
towns, sometimes in the deserts of Tartary. It is easy to
comprehend that this independent course of life had not
tended to modify the natural asperity of his character. His
intellect was entirely uncultivated; but his muscular power
was enormous, and he was not a little vain of this quality,

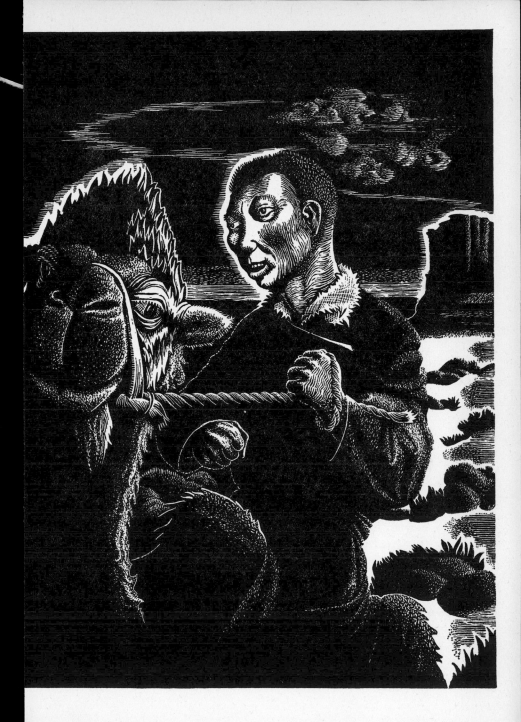

which he took great pleasure in parading. After having been instructed and baptized by Father Gabet, he had attached himself to the service of the missioners. The journey we were now undertaking was perfectly in harmony with his erratic and adventurous taste. He was, however, of no service to us as a guide across the deserts of Tartary, for he knew no more of the country than we ourselves did. Our only informants were a compass and the excellent map of the Chinese Empire by Andriveau-Goujon.

The first part of our journey was accomplished without interruption. After a toilsome climb of nearly three hours, we found ourselves at the summit of a mountain, upon an immense plateau, from which we could discern, afar off on the plains of Tartary, the tents of the Mongols, looking like so many beehives. The sun set before we had traversed this great plain, so we resolved to encamp for the night. Our first business was to seek a place providing the three essentials of fuel, water, and pasturage. The idea of robbers haunted us incessantly, and we took everybody we saw to be a suspicious character, against whom we must be on our guard. A grassy nook, surrounded by tall trees, fulfilled our requirements. Unloading our camels, we raised, with no slight labor, our tent beneath the foliage. At the tent's entrance we installed our faithful porter, Arsalan, a dog whose size, strength, and courage well entitled him to his appellation, which, in the Tartar-Mongol dialect, means "Lion."

After we collected some dry branches and *argols* (dried dung) for fuel, our kettle was soon boiling. Into the pot we threw *kouamien*, a prepared paste something like vermicelli. This, seasoned with some parings of bacon which had been given to us by our friends at Yang-pa-erh, would, we hoped, furnish satisfaction for the hunger that began to gnaw us. When the repast was ready, each of us, drawing from his girdle his wooden cup, filled it with *kouamien*, and raised it to his lips. The preparation was detestable—uneatable! The manufacturers of *kouamien* always salt it for its longer preservation, but this paste of ours had been salted beyond all endurance. Even Arsalan would not eat the composition. After soaking it for a while in cold water, we once more boiled it, but in vain; the dish remained nearly as salty as ever. So, abandoning it to Arsalan and to Samdadchiemba, whose stomach by long use was capable of anything, we were fain to content ourselves with the "dry cold," as the Chinese say.

Taking with us a couple of small loaves, we walked into the forest, in order at least to season our repast with an agreeable walk. Our first nomad supper, however, turned out better than we had expected, Providence placing in our path numerous fruit-bearing bushes. One, a shrub about five inches high, bears a pleasant wild cherry; another, also a low but very bushy shrub, produces a small scarlet apple, of a sharp, agreeable flavor, from which a very succulent jelly is made.

Deer of all kinds abound in the forest; and tigers, bears, wild boars, panthers, and wolves are scarcely less numerous. Woe to the hunters and woodcutters who venture otherwise than in large parties into the recesses of the forest: they disappear, leaving no vestige behind. The fear of encountering one of these wild beasts kept us from prolonging our walk. Besides, night was setting in, so we hastened back to our tent.

2
Fellow Nomads

HARDLY were we settled for the night, when suddenly Arsalan warned us, by his barking, of the approach of some stranger. We soon heard the trot of a horse, and presently a mounted Tartar appeared at the door. *"Mendou!"* he exclaimed, by way of respectful salutation to the supposed lamas, at the same time raising his joined hands to his forehead. When we invited him to drink a cup of tea with us, he fastened his horse to one of the tent pegs, and seated himself by the hearth. "Sirs Lamas," said he, "under what quarter of the heavens were you born?"

"We are from the western heaven. And you, whence come you?"

"My poor abode is toward the north, at the end of the valley you see there on our right."

"Your country is a fine country." The Mongol shook his head sadly, and made no reply.

"Brother," we proceeded, after a moment's silence, "the Land of Grass is still very extensive in the kingdom of Keshikten. Would it not be better to cultivate your plains? What good are these bare lands to you? Would not fine crops of corn be preferable to mere grass?"

He replied, with a tone of deep and settled conviction: "We Mongols are formed for living in tents and pasturing cattle. So long as we kept to that in the kingdom of Keshikten, we were rich and happy. Now, ever since the Mongols

7

have set themselves to cultivating the land and building houses, they have become poor." So saying, the Mongol rose, bowed, mounted his horse, and rapidly disappeared in the desert.

We traveled two more days through this kingdom, and everywhere witnessed the poverty and wretchedness of its scattered inhabitants. Yet the country is naturally endowed with astonishing wealth, especially in gold and silver mines. We left the kingdom of Keshikten, and entered that of Chahar. On the second day, when the hour of repose had arrived, we turned aside and ensconced ourselves between two rocks, where we found just space enough for our tent.

We had scarcely set up our temporary abode, when we observed, in the distance, on the slope of the mountains, a numerous body of horsemen at full gallop. Their rapid but irregular evolutions seemed to indicate that they were pursuing something which constantly evaded them. By and by, two of the horsemen, perceiving us, dashed up to our tent, dismounted, and threw themselves on the ground at the door. They were Tartar-Mongols. "Men of prayer," said they, with voices full of emotion, "we come to ask you to cast our horoscope. We have this day had two horses stolen from us. We have fruitlessly sought traces of the robbers, and we therefore come to you, men whose power and learning is beyond all limit, to tell us where we shall find our property."

"Brothers," said we, "we are not lamas of Buddha. We do not believe in horoscopes. For a man to say that he can, by any such means, discover that which is stolen, is for him to put forth words of falsehood and deception." The poor Tartars redoubled their solicitations; but when they found that we were inflexible in our resolution, they remounted their horses in order to return to the mountains.

Samdadchiemba, meanwhile, had been silent, apparently paying no attention to the incident, but sitting at the fireplace with his bowl of tea to his lips. All of a sudden he knitted his brows, rose, and came to the door. The horsemen were at some distance; but the Dchiahour, by an exertion of his strong lungs, induced them to turn round in their saddles. He motioned to them, and they, supposing we had relented and were willing to cast the desired horoscope, galloped once more towards us. When they had come within speaking distance, Samdadchiemba addressed them. "My Mongol brothers," he cried, "in future be more careful. Watch your herds well, and you won't be robbed. Retain these words of mine on your memory; they are worth all the horoscopes in the world."

After this friendly address, he gravely re-entered the tent and, seating himself at the hearth, resumed his tea. We were at first somewhat disconcerted by this singular proceeding; but as the horsemen themselves did not take the matter in ill part, but quietly rode off, we burst into a laugh.

"Stupid Mongols!" grumbled Samdadchiemba. "They don't give themselves the trouble to watch their animals, and then, when the beasts are stolen from them, they run about wanting people to cast horoscopes for them. After all, perhaps, it's no wonder, for nobody but ourselves tells them the truth. The lamas encourage them in their credulity and turn it into a source of income. It is difficult to deal with such people. If you tell them you can't cast a horoscope, they don't believe you, and merely suppose you don't choose to oblige them. To get rid of them, the best way is to give them an answer haphazard." And here Samdadchiemba laughed, with such expansion that his little eyes were completely buried.

"Did you ever cast a horoscope?" we asked.

"Yes," replied he, still laughing. "I was very young at the time, not more than fifteen. I was traveling through The Red Banner of Chahar, when I was addressed by some Mongols, who led me into their tent. There they entreated me to tell them, by means of divination, where a bull had strayed, which had been missing for three days. It was to no purpose that I protested to them I could not perform divination, that I could not even read. 'You deceive us,' said they; 'you are a Dchiahour, and we know that the western lamas can all divine, more or less.'

"As the only way of extricating myself from the dilemma, I resolved to imitate what I had seen lamas do in their divinations. I directed one person to collect eleven sheep's droppings, the driest he could find. They were immediately brought. I then seated myself very gravely; I counted the droppings over and over; I arranged them in rows, and then counted them again; I rolled them up and down in threes; and then appeared to meditate. At last I said to the Mongols, who were impatiently awaiting the result of the horoscope, 'If you would find your bull, go seek him towards the north.'

"Before the words were well out of my mouth, four men were on horseback, galloping off towards the north. By the most curious chance in the world, they had not proceeded far when the missing animal made its appearance, quietly browsing. I at once got the character of a diviner of the first class, was entertained in the most liberal manner for a week, and, when I departed, had a stock of butter and tea given me enough for another week. Now that I belong to Holy Church, I know that these things are wicked and prohibited; otherwise I would have given these horsemen a word or two of horoscope, which perhaps would have procured for us, in return, a good cup of tea with butter."

The stolen horses made us feel uneasy, and we felt ourselves obliged to take additional precautions. Before nightfall we brought in the horse and the mule and fastened them by cords to pins at the door of our tent, and then made the camels kneel by their side, so as to close up the entrance. By this arrangement no one could get near us without our having full warning given us by the camels, for these beasts, at the least noise, always make an outcry loud enough to awaken the deepest sleeper. Finally, having suspended from one of the tent poles our traveling lantern, which we kept burning all the night, we endeavored to obtain a little repose, but in vain; the night passed away without our getting a wink of sleep. As to the Dchiahour, whom nothing ever troubled, we heard him snoring with all the might of his lungs until daybreak.

We made our preparations for departure very early, for we were eager to reach Dolon-nor, which was now distant only a few leagues. On our way thither, a horseman stopped his galloping steed, and, after looking at us for a moment, addressed us: "You are the chiefs of the Christians of the Twin Ravines?"

Upon our replying in the affirmative, he dashed off again; but turned his head once or twice, to have another look at us. He was a Mongol who had charge of some herds at the Twin Ravines. He had often seen us there; but the novelty of our present costume at first prevented his recognizing us. We met also the Tartars who, the day before, had asked us to cast a horoscope for them. They had repaired by daybreak to the horse fair at Dolon-nor, in the hope of finding their stolen animals; but their search had been unsuccessful.

3
Desert Town

THE increasing number of travelers, Tartars and
Chinese, whom we now met, indicated our approach to the great town of Dolon-nor. Soon
we saw in the distance, glittering under the sun's rays, the
gilt roofs of two magnificent lamaseries that stand in the
northern suburbs of the town. We journeyed for some time
through a succession of cemeteries; for here, as elsewhere,
the present generation is surrounded by the ornamental
sepulchers of past generations. As we observed the numerous
population of that large town, hemmed in as it were by a
vast circle of bones and monumental stones, it seemed as
though death were continuously engaged in the blockade of
life.

Here and there, in the vast cemetery which completely
encircles the city, we remarked little gardens where, by dint
of extreme labor, a few miserable vegetables were extracted
from the earth: leeks, spinach, bitter lettuces, and cabbages,
which, introduced some years since from Russia, have
adapted themselves exceedingly well to the climate of
Northern China. With the exception of these few vegetables, the environs of Dolon-nor produced absolutely
nothing. The soil is dry and sandy, and water is terribly
scarce; only a few limited springs are found, and these are
dried up in the hot season.

Our entrance into the city of Dolon-nor was fatiguing and
full of perplexity, for we knew not where to take up our

12

abode. We wandered about for a long time in the labyrinth of narrow, tortuous streets, cluttered with men and animals and goods. At last we found an inn. We unloaded our camels, deposited the baggage in a small room, foddered the animals; and then, having affixed to the door of our room the padlock which, as is the custom, our landlord gave us for that purpose, we sallied forth in quest of dinner.

A triangular flag floating before a house in the next street indicated to our joyful hearts an eating-house. A long passage led us into a spacious apartment, in which were symmetrically set forth a number of little tables. When we had seated ourselves at one of these, a teapot, the inevitable prelude in these countries to every meal, was set before each of us. The guest must swallow infinite tea, and that boiling hot, before these Orientals will consent to bring him anything else. At last, when they see him thus occupied, the Controller of the Table pays his visit.

This official is a personage of immensely elegant manners and ceaseless volubility of tongue. After entertaining the guests with his views upon the affairs of the world in general, and each country in particular, he concludes by announcing what there is to eat, and requesting his hearer's judgment thereupon. As the guest mentions the dishes he desires, the Controller repeats their names in a measured chant, for the information of the Governor of the Pot. The dinner is served with admirable promptitude; but, before the guest begins the meal, etiquette requires that he rise from his seat and invite all the company present to partake. "Come," he says, with an engaging gesture, "come my friends! Come and drink a glass of wine with me; come and eat a plate of rice"—and so on.

"No, thank you," replies each one; "do you rather come and seat yourself at my table. It is I who invite you." And so the matter ends. By this ceremony the guest has "manifested his honor," as the phrase runs, and he may now sit down and eat in comfort, his character as a gentleman perfectly established.

When the guest rises to depart, the Controller of the Table again appears. As the guest crosses the apartment with him, he chants over again the names of the dishes that have been had, this time appending the prices and terminating with the sum total, announced with especial emphasis. The guest, proceeding to the counter, then deposits this sum in the money box. In general, the Chinese restaurateurs are quite as skillful as those of France in exciting the vanity of the guests and in promoting the consumption of their commodities.

Two motives had induced us to direct our steps, in the first instance, to Dolon-nor. We desired to make more purchases there to complete our traveling equipment; and, secondly, it appeared to us necessary to place ourselves in communication with the lamas of the country, in order to obtain information from them as to the more important localities of Tartary.

Dolon-nor is not a walled city, but a vast agglomeration of hideous houses, which seem to have been thrown together with a pitchfork. The purchases we needed to make gave us occasion to visit the different quarters of the town. The carriage portion of the streets is a marsh of mud and putrid filth, deep enough to stifle and bury the smaller beasts of burden that not infrequently fall within it. The carcasses of these animals remain to aggravate the general stench, while their loads become the prey of the innumerable thieves who are ever on the alert. The footpath is a narrow, rugged, slippery line on either side, just wide enough to admit the passage of one person.

Yet, despite the nastiness of the town itself, the sterility of the environs, the excessive cold of its winter, and the intolerable heat of its summer, its population is immense and its commerce enormous. Russian merchandise is brought hither in large quantities by the way of Kiakta. The Tartars bring incessant herds of camels, oxen, and horses, and carry back in exchange tobacco, linen, and tea. This constant arrival and departure of strangers communicates to the city an animated and varied aspect. All sorts of hawkers are at every corner, offering their petty wares; the regular traders, from behind their counters, with honeyed words and tempting offers, invite the passers-by to come in and buy. The lamas, in their red and yellow robes, gallop up and down, seeking admiration for the skillful management of their fiery steeds.

The magnificent statues in bronze and brass, which issue from the great foundries of Dolon-nor, are celebrated not only throughout Tartary, but in the remotest districts of Tibet. Its immense workshops supply to all the countries subject to the worship of Buddha the idols, bells, and vases employed in that idolatry. While we were in the town, a monster statue of Buddha, a present for the Grand Lama of Tibet, was packed on the backs of eighty-four camels. The larger statues are cast in detail, the component parts being afterward soldered together.

We availed ourselves of our stay at Dolon-nor to have a figure of Christ constructed, on the model of a bronze original which we had brought with us from France. The workmen so marvelously excelled, that it was difficult to distinguish the copy from the original. The artisans of Tartary work rapidly and cheaply, and their willingness to please contrasts most favorably with the stubbornness of certain European artists.

During our stay at Dolon-nor, we had frequent occasion to visit the lamaseries, or lama monasteries, and to converse with the priests of Buddha. The lamas appeared to us persons of very limited information; and as to their symbolism, in general, it is little more refined or purer than the creed of the vulgar. Their doctrine is still undecided, fluctuating amidst a vast pantheism of which they can give no intelligible account. When we asked them for some distinct, clear, positive idea of what they meant, they were always thrown into utter embarrassment, and stared at one another. The disciples told us that their masters knew all about it; the masters referred us to the omniscience of the Grand Lamas; the Grand Lamas confessed themselves ignorant, but talked of some wonderful saint in some lamasery at the other end of the country: *he* could explain the whole affair.

However, all of them, disciples and masters, great lamas and small, agreed in this, that their doctrine came from the west. "The nearer you approach the west," said they unanimously, "the purer and more luminous will the doctrine show itself to be." When we expounded to them the truths of Christianity, they never discussed the matter. They contented themselves with calmly saying: "Well, we don't suppose that our prayers are the only prayers in the world. The lamas of the west will explain everything to you. We believe in the traditions that have come from the west."

In point of fact, there is no lamasery of any importance in Tartary, the Grand Lama or superior of which is not a man from Tibet. Any Tartar lama who has visited Lhasa (Land of Spirits), or Monke-jot (Eternal Sanctuary) as it is called in the Mongol dialect, is received, on his return, as a man to whom the mysteries of the past and of the future have been unveiled.

4

Into the West

AFTER maturely weighing the information we
had obtained from the lamas, we decided to
direct our steps towards the west. On the first
of October we quitted Dolon-nor; and it was not without
infinite trouble that we managed to traverse the filthy town
with our camels. The poor animals could get through the
quagmire streets only by fits and starts: it was first a stumble,
then a convulsive jump, then another stumble and another
jump, and so on. Their loads shook on their backs, and at
every step we expected to see camel and camel-load prostrate
in the mud. We considered ourselves lucky when, at distant
intervals, we came to a comparatively dry spot where the
camels could travel, and we were thus enabled to readjust
and tighten our baggage. Samdadchiemba got into a des-
perate ill temper; he went on, and slipped, and went on
again, without uttering a single word, restricting the visible
manifestation of his wrath to a continuous biting of the lips.

Upon attaining at length the western extremity of the
town, we got clear of the filth indeed, but found ourselves
involved in another evil. Before us there was no road marked
out, not the slightest trace of even a path. There was nothing
but an apparently interminable chain of small hills, composed of fine, moving sand, over which it was impossible to
advance at more than a snail's pace, and this only with extreme labor. Among these sand hills, moreover, we were
oppressed with an absolutely stifling heat. Our animals were

covered with sweat; ourselves devoured with a burning thirst. But it was in vain that we looked around in all directions for water; not a spring, not a pool, not a drop presented itself.

It was already late, and we began to fear we should find no spot favorable for the erection of our tent. The ground, however, grew firmer by degrees, and we at last discerned some signs of vegetation. By and by the sand almost disappeared, and our eyes rejoiced at the sight of continuous verdure. On our left, at no great distance, we saw the opening of a ravine. Father Gabet urged on his camel and went to examine the spot. He soon made his appearance at the summit of a hill, and with voice and hand directed us to follow him. We hastened on and found that Providence had led us to a favorable position. A small pool—the waters of which were half concealed by thick reeds and other marshy vegetation—some brushwood, a plot of grass: under the circumstances what more could we desire? Hungry, thirsty, weary as we were, the place seemed to us a perfect Eden.

The camels were no sooner squatted, than we all three, with one accord and without a word, seized each man his wooden cup, and rushed to the pond to satisfy his thirst. The water was fresh enough; but it affected the nose violently with its strong hydro-sulphuric odor. I remembered having drunk water just like it in the Pyrenees, at the good town of Aix, and to have seen it for sale in the chemists' shops elsewhere in France; and I remembered also that it sold for at least fifteen sous a bottle—it was so stinking and nauseating.

After we had quenched our thirst, our strength by degrees returned. We were able to fix our tent, and then each man set about his special task. Father Gabet proceeded to cut some bundles of horn-beam wood; Samdadchiemba collected *argols* in the flap of his jacket; and Father Huc, seated at the entrance of the tent, tried his hand at drawing a fowl—a process which Arsalan, stretched at his side, watched with greedy eye, having immediate reference to the entrails

in course of removal. We were resolved, for once, to have a
little festival in the desert, and to take the opportunity to
indulge our patriotism by initiating our Dchiahour in the
luxury of a dish prepared according to the rules of the
French cuisine.

The fowl, artistically dismembered, was placed at the
bottom of our great pot. A few roots of synapia, prepared
in salt water, some onions, a clove of garlic, and some all-
spice, constituted the seasoning. The preparation was soon
boiling, for we were that day rich in fuel. By and by Samdadchiemba plunged in his hand and drew out a limb of the
fowl, and, after carefully inspecting it, pronounced supper
to be ready. Upon the grass we placed the pot, and all three
of us seated ourselves around so that our knees almost
touched it; then each one, armed with two chopsticks,
fished out the pieces he desired from the abundant broth
before him. When this meal was completed, and we had
thanked God for the repast He had thus provided for us in
the desert, Samdadchiemba went and washed the caldron
in the pond; then he brewed us some tea.

Tartar tea is not prepared in the same way as that used by
the Chinese. The latter select only the smaller and tenderer
leaves of the plant, which they simply infuse in boiling
water, so as to give it a golden tint. The coarser leaves, with
which are mixed the smaller tendrils, are set aside for Tartar
tea. This mixture is pressed together in a mold, in the form
and size of the ordinary house brick. When required for
use, a piece of the brick is broken off, pulverized, and boiled
in the kettle, until the water assumes a reddish hue. Some
salt is then thrown in, and effervescence commences. When
the liquid has become almost black, milk is added, and the
beverage, the grand luxury of the Tartars, is then transferred
to the teapot. Samdadchiemba was wildly enthusiastic about
this tea. For our part, we drank it in default of something
better.

Next morning, after rolling up our tent, we quitted this

haven. Before departing, we set up, as an *ex voto* of our gratitude for its hospitality to us for a night, a small wooden cross on the site of our fireplace; and this precedent we afterwards followed at all our camping places. Could missioners leave a more appropriate memorial of their journey through the desert!

The weather was magnificent. By degrees, the coarse grass of the prairie raised its strong head, which had been depressed by the heavy rain; the ground became firmer, and we experienced with delight the gentle heat of the sun's rays. At last, to complete our satisfaction, we entered upon the plains of The Red Banner, the most picturesque part of the whole of the kingdom of Chahar. We had never traversed a more beautiful country. The desert is at times horrible, hideous; but it also has its charms—charms all the more intensely appreciated because they are rare in themselves, and because they would be sought in vain in populated countries.

Tartary has an aspect altogether peculiar: there is nothing in the rest of the world that at all resembles a Tartar landscape. In civilized countries the traveler finds at every step populous towns, rich and varied cultivation, the thousand and one productions of arts and industry, the incessant movements of commerce. He is constantly impelled onwards, carried away, as it were, by some vast whirlwind. On the other hand, in countries where civilization has not as yet made headway, the traveler finds nothing but primeval forests in all the pomp of their exuberant and gigantic vegetation; and the soul seems crushed beneath nature all powerful and majestic. There is nothing of either kind in Tartary. There are no towns, no edifices, no arts, no industry, no cultivation, no forests; everywhere it is open, unsettled country, sometimes broken by immense lakes, by majestic rivers, by rugged and imposing mountains; sometimes spreading out into vast limitless plains.

5

Tartar Hospitality

AFTER having journeyed the entire day through the delightful prairies of The Red Banner, we halted to encamp for the night in a valley that seemed full of people. We had scarcely alighted, when a number of Tartars approached and offered their services. After having assisted us to unload our camels and set up our house of blue linen, they invited us to come and take tea in their tents. As it was late, however, we stayed at home, promising to pay them a visit next morning; for the hospitable invitation of our new neighbors determined us to remain for a day amongst them. We were, moreover, very well pleased to profit by the beauty of the weather and of the locality, to recover from the fatigue we had undergone the day before.

Next morning, the time not required for our little household cares and the recitation of our Breviary was devoted to visiting the Mongol tents (Samdadchiemba was left at home in charge of our own tent). Our first care had to be for the safety of our legs, which were menaced by a whole host of watchdogs. A small stick apiece sufficed for the purpose; but Tartar etiquette required us to leave these weapons at the threshold of our host's abode. To enter a man's tent with a whip or a stick in one's hand is as great an insult as one can offer to the family, and quite tantamount to saying, "You are all dogs."

Among the Tartars, visiting is a frank, simple affair, altogether exempt from the endless formalities of Chinese gentility. On entering, the visitor gives the word of peace, *Amor* or *Mendou*, to the company generally. He then seats himself at the right of the head of the family, who are all squatting on the floor opposite the entrance. Next, each man takes from a purse suspended at his girdle a little snuff bottle, and mutual pinches accompany such queries as these:

"Is the pasturage with you rich and abundant?"
"Are your herds in fine condition?"
"Are your mares productive?"
"Did you travel in peace?"
"Does tranquillity prevail?"

And so on. These questions and their answers are always interchanged with intense gravity on both sides. Then the mistress of the tent, without saying a word, holds out her hand to the visitor. He as silently takes from his breast pocket the small wooden bowl, the indispensable *vade mecum* of all Tartars, and presents it to his hostess, who fills it with tea and milk and returns it.

In the richer, more comfortable families, visitors have a small table placed before them, on which are butter, oatmeal, grated millet, and bits of cheese, each food separately contained in its own little box of polished wood. These Tartar delicacies the visitors take mixed with their tea. Those hosts who propose to treat their guests in a style of perfect magnificence make them partakers of a bottle of Mongol wine, warmed in the ashes. This wine is nothing more than skimmed milk, subjected for awhile to fermentation and then distilled. One must be a thorough Tartar to relish or even endure this beverage, the flavor and odor of which are alike insipid.

The two days we passed in these fine plains of Chahar were not without profit. We were able at leisure to repair our clothes and our baggage; but, above all, we had an opportunity to study the Tartars close at hand, and to initiate

ourselves in the habits of the nomad peoples. As we were
making preparations for departure, these temporary neighbors aided us to fold our tent and to load our camels. "Sirs
Lamas," said they, "you had better encamp to-night at
The Three Lakes; the pasturage there is good and abundant.
If you make haste, you will reach the place before sunset.
On this side and on the other side of The Three Lakes,
there is no water for a considerable distance. Sirs Lamas, a
good journey to you!"

"Peace be with you, and farewell!" responded we; and
with that we proceeded once more on our way, Samdadchiemba heading the caravan, mounted on his little black
mule. We quitted this encampment without regret, just as
we had quitted preceding encampments; except, indeed,
that here we left, on the spot where our tent had stood, a
greater heap of ashes, and that the grass around it was more
trodden than was usual with us.

It was past noon when we came to a place where three
wells had been dug, at short distances from each other. Although the day was still young, we thought it best to encamp. For a vast plain, on which we could discern no sort
of habitation, stretched out before us to the distant horizon;
and we might fairly conclude it to be destitute of water,
since the Tartars had taken the trouble to dig these wells.

We therefore set up our tent. But we soon found that
we had selected a detestable location. With the excessive nastiness of very brackish and very fetid water was combined
extreme scarcity of fuel. We looked about for *argols*, but
in vain. At last Samdadchiemba, whose eyes were better
than ours, discerned in the distance a sort of enclosure, in
which he concluded that cattle had been folded. He took
a camel with him to the place in the hope of finding plenty
of *argols* there, and he certainly returned with an ample
supply. But unfortunately the precious fuel was not dry.

The Dchiahour essayed an experiment. He hollowed out
a sort of furnace in the ground, surmounting it with a turf

chimney. The structure was extremely picturesque, but it labored under the enormous disadvantage of being wholly useless. Samdadchiemba arranged and rearranged his fuel, and puffed and puffed with all the force of his potent lungs. It was all lost labor. There was smoke enough, and to spare; we were enveloped in smoke. But there was no spark of fire, and the water in the kettle remained relentlessly passive. It was obvious that to boil our tea or heat oatmeal was out of the question. Yet we were anxious, at all events, to take the chill off the water, and to disguise, by the warmth, its brackish flavor and its disagreeable smell. So we adopted the following expedient.

On the plains of Mongolia one sees little animals like gray squirrels, which live in holes, as do rats. These animals construct, over the opening of their little dens, miniature domes, composed of grass, artistically twisted, and designed as shelter from wind and rain. These little heaps of dry grass are the form and size of mole hills. The place where we had now set up our tent abounded with these gray squirrels. Thirst made us cruel, and we proceeded to level the house domes of these poor little animals, which retreated into their holes below as we approached them. By means of this vandalism we managed to collect a sackful of satisfactory fuel, and so warmed the water of the well, which was our only refreshment during the day.

Our provisions had materially diminished, notwithstanding the economy to which the want of fire on this and other occasions had reduced us. There remained very little meal or millet in our bags, when we learned, from a Tartar whom we met on the way, that we were at no great distance from a trading station called Shabartai (Slough). It lay, indeed, somewhat out of the route we were pursuing; but there was no other place at which we could supply ourselves with provisions until we should come to Blue Town, from which we were distant a hundred leagues. We turned therefore to the left, and soon reached Shabartai.

6
Mongol Customs

WE arrived at Shabartai on the fifteenth day of the eighth moon, an anniversary of great rejoicing among the Chinese. This festival, known as the *Yüeh Ping* (Loaves of the Moon), dates from the remotest antiquity. Its original purpose was to honor the moon with superstitious rites. On this solemn day all labor is suspended; the workmen receive from their employers a present of money; every person puts on his best clothes; and there is merrymaking in every family. Relations and friends interchange cakes of various sizes, on each of which is stamped the sign of the moon; that is to say, a hare crouching amid a small group of trees.

Since the fourteenth century this festival has borne a political character, little understood, apparently, by the Mongols, but carefully perpetuated by the Chinese. About the year 1368, the Chinese were desirous of shaking off the yoke of the Tartar dynasty, which had been founded by Genghis Khan and had then swayed the empire for nearly a hundred years. A vast conspiracy was formed throughout all the provinces: on the fifteenth day of the eighth moon there was to be a general massacre of the Mongol soldiers, who were billeted with every Chinese family for the double purpose of maintaining themselves and their conquest. The signal for the massacre was given by letters concealed in the cakes which were on that day mutually interchanged throughout the country. The massacre was effected, and the Tartar army scattered in the houses of the Chinese was utterly annihilated.

This uprising put an end to the Mongol domination; and ever since, the Chinese, in celebrating the festival of *Yüeh Ping,* have been less intent upon the superstitious worship of the moon than upon the tragic event to which they owed the recovery of their national independence. The Mongols, however, seem to have entirely lost all memory of the sanguinary revolution: every year they take their full part in the festival of the Loaves of the Moon, and thus celebrate, without apparently knowing it, the triumph which their enemies heretofore gained over their ancestors.

Within gunshot of the place where we were encamped, we perceived several Mongol tents, the size and character of which indicated easy circumstances on the part of the proprietors. This indication was confirmed by the large herds of cattle, sheep, and horses, which were pasturing around. While we were reciting the Breviary in our tent, Samdadchiemba went to pay a visit to these Mongols. Soon afterwards we saw approaching an old man with a long white beard and features which bespoke him a personage of distinction. He was accompanied by a young lama, and by a little boy who held his hand.

"Sirs Lamas," said the old man, "all men are brothers; but they who dwell in tents are united one with another as flesh with bone. Sirs Lamas, will you come and seat yourselves awhile in my poor abode? The fifteenth of this moon is a solemn epoch; you are strangers and travelers, and therefore cannot this evening occupy your places at the hearth of your own noble family. Come and repose for a few days with us; your presence will bring us peace and happiness."

We told the good old man that we could not wholly accept his offer, but that in the evening, after prayers, we would come and take tea with him and converse for a while about the Mongol nation. The venerable Tartar hereupon took his leave. But he had not been gone long, before the young lama who had accompanied him returned and told us that his people were awaiting our presence. We felt that we could not refuse to comply at once with an invitation so full of frank cordiality; and accordingly, having directed our Dchiahour to take good care of our tent, we followed the young lama who had come in quest of us.

Upon entering the Mongol tent, we were astonished to find a cleanliness one is little accustomed to meet in Tartary. There was not the ordinary coarse fireplace in the center, and the eye was not offended with the dirty, rude kitchen utensils which generally encumber Tartar habitations. It was obvious, besides, that everything had been prepared for a festival. We seated ourselves upon a large red carpet; and there was almost immediately brought to us from the adjacent tent, which served as a kitchen, some tea with milk; some small loaves fried in butter; and cheese, raisins, and jujubes.

After we had been introduced to the numerous Mongols by whom we found ourselves surrounded, the conversation insensibly turned upon the festival of the Loaves of the Moon. "In our western land," said we, "this festival is unknown. Men there adore only God, the Creator of the heavens, of the earth, of the sun, of the moon, and of all that exists."

"Oh, what a holy doctrine!" exclaimed the old man, raising his clasped hands to his forehead. "The Tartars themselves, for that matter, do not worship the moon; but, seeing that the Chinese celebrate this festival, they follow the custom without very well knowing why."

"You say truly: you do not, indeed, know why you celebrate this festival. That is what we heard in the land of the Chinese. But do you know why the Chinese celebrate it?" Thereupon we related to these Mongols what we knew of the terrible massacre of their ancestors.

Upon the completion of our narrative, we saw the faces

of all our audience full of astonishment. The young men whispered to one another. The old man preserved a mournful silence; his head was bent down, and big tears flowed from his eyes. "Brother rich in years," said we, "this story does not seem to surprise you as it does your young men, but it fills your heart with emotion."

"Holy personages," replied the elder, raising his head and wiping away the tears with the back of his hand, "the terrible event—the story of which occasions such consternation in the minds of my young men—was not unknown to me, but I would I had never heard of it! I always struggle against its recollection, for it brings the hot blood into the forehead of every Tartar whose heart is not sold to the Chinese. A day known to our great lamas will come, when the blood of our fathers, so shamefully assassinated, will at length be avenged. When the holy man who is to lead us to vengeance shall appear, every one of us will rise and follow in his train; then we will march, in the face of day, and require from the Chinese an account of the Tartar blood which they shed in the silence and dark secrecy of their houses. The Mongols celebrate every year this festival, most of them seeing in it merely an indifferent ceremony; but the Loaves of the Moon Day ever recall, in the hearts of a few amongst us, the memory of the treachery to which our fathers fell victims, and the hope of just vengeance."

After a brief silence, the old man went on: "Holy personages, whatever may be the associations of this day, in other respects it is truly a festival for us, since you have deigned to enter our poor habitation. Let us not further occupy our breasts with sad thoughts. Child," said he to a young man seated on the threshold of the tent, "if the mutton is boiled enough, clear away these things."

This command having been executed, the eldest son of the family entered, bearing in both hands a small oblong table, on which was a boiled sheep, cut into four quarters, heaped one on the other. The family being assembled round the table, the chief drew a knife from his girdle, severed the sheep's tail, and divided it into two equal pieces, which he placed before us. With the Tartars, the tail is considered the most delicious portion of their sheep, and accordingly the most honorable. These tails of the Tartar sheep are of immense size and weight, the fat upon them alone weighing from six to eight pounds. We did our best to do justice to these Tartar delicacies, to which we were not accustomed. However, we did enjoy without any pretense the kindly hospitality of these good folk, and we counted the hours spent with them as well worth while, since we were acquiring a better knowledge of the Tartar language and customs.

The day after the festival, the sun had scarcely risen when a little boy presented himself at the entrance of our tent, carrying in one hand a wooden vessel full of milk, and in the other a rude rush basket, in which were some new cheese and some butter. He was followed soon after by an old lama, attended by a Tartar who had on his shoulder a large bag of fuel. We invited them all to be seated. "Brothers of the west," said the lama, "accept these trifling presents from my master."

We bowed in token of thanks, and Samdadchiemba hastened to prepare some tea, for which we pressed the lama to stay. "I will come and see you this evening," said he; "but I cannot remain at present, for I have not set my pupil the prayer he has to learn this morning."

The pupil in question was the little boy who had brought the milk. The old man then took his pupil by the hand, and they returned together to their tent. The old lama was the family tutor, and his occupation consisted in directing the little boy in the study of the Tibetan prayers.

The education of Tartars is very limited. They who shave the head—the lamas—are, as a general rule, the only persons who learn to read and pray. There is no such thing throughout the country as a public school. With the exception of

a few rich Mongols who have their children taught at home,
all send their young sons to the lamaseries, wherein is con-
centrated all that exists in Tartary of art, or science, or intellectual industry. The lama is not merely a priest: he is
the painter, poet, sculptor, architect, physician; the head,
heart, and oracle of the laity.

The training of the Mongol boys who do not resort to
the lamaseries is restricted to learning the use of the bow
and arrow and matchlock, and to obtaining a thorough
mastery of equestrianism. When a mere infant, the Mongol
is weaned; and as soon as he is strong enough, he is stuck
upon a horse's back behind a man, the animal is put to a
gallop, and the juvenile rider, in order not to fall off, has
to cling with both hands to his teacher's jacket. Tartars
thus become accustomed, from a very early age, to the
movements of the horse, and soon by force of habit they
identify themselves, as it were, with the animal.

There is, perhaps, no spectacle more exciting than that
of Mongol riders in pursuit of a wild horse. Each man is
armed with a long, heavy pole, at the end of which is a
running knot. The riders gallop, they seem to fly, after the
horse they are pursuing, down rugged ravines and up precip-
itous hills, in and out, twisting and twining in their rapid
course, until they come up with their game. Each horseman then takes the bridle of his own horse in his teeth,
seizes with both hands his heavy pole, and, bending forward, tries to throw, by a powerful effort, the running knot
round the wild horse's neck. In this exercise the greatest
vigor must be combined with the greatest dexterity, in order
to enable the riders to stop short the powerful, untamed
animals with which they have to deal. It sometimes happens
that pole and cord are broken; but as to a horseman being
thrown, that is an occurrence we never heard of or saw.

The Mongol is so accustomed to horseback that he is
altogether like a fish out of water when he sets foot on the
ground. His step is heavy and awkward; and his bowed

legs, his chest bent forward, his constant looking around him, all indicate a person who spends the greater portion of his time on the back of a horse or a camel. When night overtakes the traveling Tartar, it often happens that he will not even take the trouble to alight for the purpose of repose. If we asked people whom we met in the desert where they slept the preceding night, we frequently received, in a melancholy tone, the answer, "*Temen dero* (On the camel)." Caravans halting at noon, when they come to a rich pasturage, present a striking spectacle: the camels disperse in all directions, browsing upon the high grass of the prairie, while the Tartars, astride between the two humps of the animals, sleep as profoundly as though they were sheltered in good beds.

7

Stray Animals and a Temple

ON the seventeenth of the moon, we proceeded, very early in the morning, to the Chinese town of Shabartai, for the purpose of laying in a store of meal. Shabartai, as its Mongol name intimates, is built upon a slough. The houses are all made of mud, and each is surrounded by an enclosure of high walls. The streets are irregular, tortuous, and narrow; the aspect of the whole settlement is somber and sinister. The trade of the town includes all the articles in ordinary use with the Mongols—oatmeal and millet, cotton manufactures, and brick tea. These the Tartars receive in exchange for their own products of the desert—salt, mushrooms, and furs.

After making our purchases, we returned and hastened to prepare for departure. While we were packing our baggage in the tent, Samdadchiemba went in search of the animals which had been put to pasture in the vicinity. A moment afterwards he returned with the three camels. "There are the camels," said we, with gloomy anticipation, "but where are the horse and mule? They were both at hand just now, for we tied their legs to prevent their straying."

"They are stolen, in all probability!" This answer came upon us like a clap of thunder. However, it was not a moment for lamentation; there was need to go at once in search of the thieves. We each mounted a camel, and made a circuit in search of the animals, leaving our tent under

the charge of Arsalan. When search proved futile, we resolved to proceed to the Mongol encampment and inform
those neighbors that the animals had been lost near their
habitation.

By a law among the Tartars, when animals are lost from
a caravan, the persons occupying the nearest encampment
are bound either to find the animals or to replace them.
It seems, no doubt, very strange to the European mind
that because, without their consent or even knowledge,
without being in the slightest degree acquainted with them,
a traveler chooses to pitch his tent near the encampment
of a Mongol party, he and his animals and his baggage become the responsibility of that party; but so it is. If anything disappears, the law supposes that the next neighbor
is the thief, or at all events an accomplice. This situation
has contributed to render the Mongols skillful in tracking
animals. A mere glance at the slight traces left upon the
grass suffices to inform the Mongol pursuer how long since
the animal passed, and whether or not it bore a rider; and
when the track is once found, it is followed throughout all
its meanderings, however complicated.

We had no sooner explained our loss to the Mongol
chief than he said to us cheerfully: "Sirs Lamas, do not
permit sorrow to invade your hearts. Your animals cannot
be lost; in these plains there are neither robbers nor associ-
ates of robbers. I will send in quest of your horses. If we
do not find them, you may select what others you please in
their place, from our herd. We would have you leave this
place as happy as you came to it."

While he was speaking, eight of his people mounted on
horseback and dashed off in as many directions upon the
quest, each man trailing after him his lasso attached to the
long flexible pole we have described. After a while they all
collected in one body and galloped away, as hard as they
could, towards the town. "They are on the track now, holy
sirs," said the chief, who was watching their movements by

our sides, "and you will have your horses back very soon. Meanwhile, come within my tent and drink some tea."

In about two hours, a boy appeared at the entrance of the tent and announced the return of the horsemen. We hastened outside and, in the track which we had followed, saw something amid a cloud of dust which seemed to be horsemen galloping like the wind. We presently perceived the eight Tartars, dashing along like so many mad centaurs, with our stray animals, each held by a lasso, in the midst of them. On their arrival they alighted, and with an air of satisfaction said, "We told you nothing was ever lost in our country!" We thanked the generous Mongols for the great service they had rendered us; then, bidding adieu to them, saddled our horses, and departed on our way.

For several days we passed through a great solitude, witnessing by the way only the ruins of a long-abandoned city and a few Mongol shepherds. Finally we came upon a green place in the hollow of a valley. The sun was on the point of setting when we pitched our tent on the margin of a stream about a hundred yards from the lamasery of Chorchi, where about two thousand lamas live. This is said to be the favorite lamasery of the Emperor, and he has loaded it with gifts and privileges.

The morning after our encampment, we spent several hours visiting the different buildings and courtyards of the lamasery of Chorchi, which we found to conform to the general plan of the Buddhist structures. It would be difficult to say to what order of architecture all these temples of Tartary belong. They are always fantastic constructions of monstrous colonnades, and peristyles of twisted columns. Opposite the great gate is a kind of altar of wood or stone, usually in the form of a cone reversed; on this the idols are placed, mostly seated cross-legged. These idols are of colossal stature, but their faces are fine and regular; except for the preposterous length of the ears, they are the Caucasian type.

Before the chief idol, and on the same level with it, is a gilt seat where the Living *Fo*, the Grand Lama of the lamasery, has his seat. All around the temple are long benches almost level with the ground, forming a sort of ottoman which is covered with carpet; and between each row there is a vacant space, so that the lamas may move about freely.

When the hour for prayer is come, a lama whose office it is to summon the guests of the convent proceeds to the great gate of the temple and blows a conch shell as loud as he can towards the four points of the compass, successively. Upon hearing this powerful instrument, which is audible for a league distant, the lamas put on the mantle and cap of ceremony and assemble in the great inner court. After a short wait, the conch shell is sounded again, the great gate is opened, and the Living *Fo* enters the temple. As soon as he is seated upon the altar, all the lamas leave their red boots in the vestibule and advance barefoot and in silence. As they pass him, they worship the Living *Fo* by three prostrations, and then place themselves upon the ottoman, each according to his dignity. They sit cross-legged, always choir-wise, that is, face to face.

As soon as the master of the ceremonies has given the signal, by tinkling a little bell, each lama murmurs in a low voice a preliminary prayer, whilst he unrolls upon his knees the service of prayers directed by the rubrics. After this short recitation, there follows a moment of profound silence; then the bell is again rung, and a psalm is begun by both sides, grave and melodious. The Tibetan prayers, ordinarily in verse, and written in a metrical and well-cadenced style, are marvelously adapted for harmony. At certain pauses, indicated by the rubric, the lama musicians execute a piece of music, little in harmony with the melodious gravity of the psalmody. It is a confused and deafening noise of bells, cymbals, tambourines, sea conches, trumpets, pipes, and so forth, each musician playing on his instrument with a kind of ecstatic fury, competing with his brethren to make the greatest noise.

The interior of the temple is usually filled with ornaments, statues, and pictures, illustrating the life of Buddha and the various transmigrations of the more illustrious lamas. Vases in copper, shining like gold, of the size and shape of teacups, are placed in great numbers on a succession of steps, in the form of an amphitheater, before the idols. It is in these vases that the people deposit their offerings of milk, butter, Mongol wine, and meal. On the extremities of each step are censers, in which are ever burning aromatic plants, gathered on the sacred mountains of Tibet. Rich silk stuffs, covered with tinsel and gold embroidery, form, over the heads of the idols, canopies from which hang pennants and lanterns of painted paper or transparent horn. The lamas are the only artists who contribute to the ornamentation of the temples, and their pictures are contrary to the taste and the canons of art as understood in Europe.

8

Provisions and a Thief

AFTER quitting the place, just as we were entering upon The Red Banner, we met a Mongol hunter, who was carrying behind him, on his horse, a fine roebuck he had just killed. We had been so long reduced to our insipid oatmeal, seasoned with a few bits of mutton fat, that the sight of the venison inspired us with a somewhat decided desire to vary our diet. We felt, moreover, that our stomachs, weakened by daily privations, imperiously demanded a more substantial fare. After saluting the hunter, therefore, we asked him if he was disposed to sell his venison.

"Sirs Lamas," replied he, "when I placed myself in ambush to await the deer, I had no thought whatever of trading. The Chinese drivers, stationed up yonder beyond Chorchi, wanted to buy my game for four hundred sapeks, but I said 'No!' But to you, Sirs Lamas, I speak not as to Chinese: there is my roebuck; give me what you please for it."

We told Samdadchiemba to pay the hunter five hundred sapeks. Five hundred sapeks are equivalent to about fifty cents, and this is the ordinary price of a roebuck in Tartary; the price of a sheep is thrice that amount. Venison is little esteemed by the Tartars, and still less by the Chinese: black meat, say they, is never so good as white. Yet in the larger cities of China, and especially at Peking, black meat has an honorable place on the tables of the rich and of the man-

darins—a circumstance to be attributed, however, to the
scarcity of the article and a desire for variety. The Manchus,
indeed, do not come within the preceding observation; for,
great lovers of hunting, they are also great lovers of its
produce, especially of bears, stags, and pheasants.

Hanging the venison over the neck of one of our camels,
we proceeded on our way. It was just past noon when we
came to a spot marvelously beautiful. After passing through
a narrow opening between two rocks, the summits of which
seemed lost in the clouds, we found ourselves in a large enclosure, surrounded by lofty hills, on which grew a number
of scattered pines. An abundant fountain supplied a small
stream, which flowed between banks covered with angelica
and wild mint. No sooner had a glance comprehended the
attractions of the spot, than Samdadchiemba suggested that
we should at once set up our tent there. "Let us go no
further today," said he; "let us encamp here. We have not
gone far this morning, it is true, and the sun is still very
high; but we have got the venison to prepare, and should
therefore encamp earlier than usual."

As no one opposed the honorable gentleman's suggestion, we proceeded to set up our tent by the side of the
spring. Samdadchiemba had often talked of his great dexterity in the dissection of animals, and he was delighted
with the opportunity of displaying his excellence in this
respect. Having suspended the roebuck from a pine branch,
sharpened his knife upon a tent pin, and turned up his
sleeves to the elbow, he asked whether we should prefer
the animal dismembered *à la Turque, à la Chinoise*, or *à la
Tartare*. Unprovided with a reason for preferring any one
of these modes, we left it to Samdadchiemba to obey the
impulse of his genius in the matter. In a minute he had
skinned and gutted the animal; then he cut away the flesh
from the bones, in one piece, without separating the limbs,
so as to leave suspended from the tree merely the skeleton
of the deer. This, it appeared, was the Turk fashion, in use

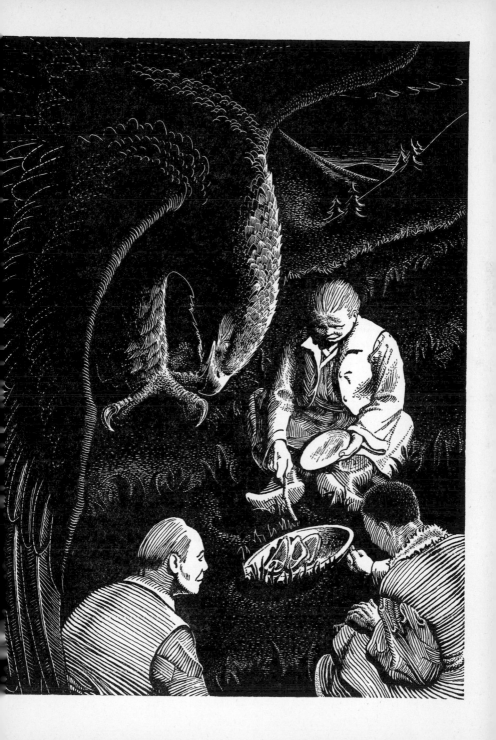

upon long journeys, in order to relieve travelers of the
useless burden of bones.

The operation completed, Samdadchiemba cut some slices
of venison and proceeded to fry them in mutton fat. This
is a manner of preparing venison not perhaps in strict accordance with the rules of culinary art, but the difficulty
of the circumstances did not allow us to do better. Our
banquet was soon ready, but, contrary to our expectations,
we were not the first to taste it. We seated ourselves on the
grass, having in our midst the lid of the pot, which served
us as a dish. All of a sudden we heard, as it were, the rush-
ing of a storm over our heads: a great eagle dashed, like a
lightning stroke, upon our dinner, and immediately rose
with equal rapidity, bearing off in each claw a large slice of
venison.

Upon recovering from our fright at this sudden incident,
we ourselves were fain to laugh at the ludicrous aspect of
the matter. But Samdadchiemba did not laugh by any
means; he was in a paroxysm of fury, not indeed at the loss
of the venison, but because the eagle, in its flight, insolently
dealt him a sound box on the ear with the extremity of its
great wing. This event served to render us more cautious
on the following venison days. During our previous journey-
ings, we had, indeed, on several occasions observed eagles
hovering over our heads at mealtimes, but no incident of
this kind had occurred; probably the royal birds had scorned
our ordinary oatmeal repasts.

One sees the eagle almost everywhere throughout the
deserts of Tartary, sometimes hovering and making large
circles in the air, sometimes perched upon rising ground,
motionless as the hillock itself. No one in these countries
hunts the eagle or molests it in any way: it may make its
nest where it pleases, and there bring up its eaglets, and itself grow old, without being in the least interfered with by
man. Often an eagle may be seen resting on the plain, and
in that position appearing to be larger than a sheep. As the

traveler approaches, it moves leisurely along the ground, beating its wings; and then, ascending by degrees, it attains the altitude where it can fly in all its grandeur and power.

9

Stay in Blue Town

AFTER several days' journey we quitted the country of The Eight Banners and entered upon the fine rolling plains of Manchuria, with cultivated fields on either hand. Here we were grateful for the luxury of spending our nights in an inn, and for the use of well-defined roads that made our going less difficult. At length we came within sight of the towering walls of the city known as Old Blue Town, an immense mass of houses and shops huddled confusedly together.

We entered into the town by a broad street, which exhibited nothing remarkable except the large lamasery, called, in common with the more celebrated establishment in the province of Shansi, the Lamasery of the Five Towers. This appellation is derived from a handsome square tower with five turrets—one, very lofty, in the center, and one at each corner.

During our short stay at Blue Town, we had constant conversation with the lamas of the most celebrated lamaseries, endeavoring to obtain fresh information on the state of Buddhism in Tartary and Tibet. All they told us only served to confirm us more and more in what we had before learnt on this subject. In Blue Town, as at Dolon-nor, every one told us that the doctrine would appear more sublime and more luminous as we advanced towards the west. From what the lamas who had visited Tibet said, Lhasa was, as it were, a great focus of light, the rays of which grew more and more feeble in proportion as they became removed from their center.

One day we had an opportunity to talk for some time with a Tibetan lama, and the things he told us about religion astounded us greatly. A brief explanation of the Christian doctrine, which we gave to him, seemed scarcely to surprise him; he even maintained that our views differed little from those of the Grand Lamas of Tibet. "You must not confound," said he, "religious truths with the superstitions of the vulgar. The Tartars, poor, simple people, prostrate themselves before whatever they see: with them everything is *Borhan*. Lamas, prayer books, temples, lamaseries, stones, heaps of bones—'tis all the same to them; down they go on their knees, crying, '*Borhan! Borhan!*' "

"But the lamas themselves admit innumerable *Borhans?*"

"Let me explain," said our friend smilingly. "There is but one sole Sovereign of the universe, the Creator of all things, without beginning and without end. In India he bears the name of Buddha; in Tibet, that of *Samtche Mitcheba* (All-Powerful Eternal); the Chinese call him *Fo*; and the Tartars call him *Borhan.*"

"You say that Buddha is the One Almighty? In that case who are the Grand Lama of Lhasa, the Bandchan of Jashilumbo, the Tsong-Kaba of the Hsi-fan, the Kaldan of Dolonnor, the Guison-Tamba of the Great Kuren, the Hobilgan of Blue Town, the Hotoktou of Peking, the Chaberon of the Tartar and Tibetan lamaseries?"

"They are all equally Buddha."

"Is Buddha visible?"

"No, he is without a body; he is a spiritual substance."

"So, Buddha is the One Almighty and yet there exist innumerable Buddhas: the Grand Lama, and so on. Buddha is incorporeal; he cannot be seen; and yet the Grand Lama, the Guison-Tamba, and the rest are visible, and have bodies like our own. How do you explain all this?"

"The doctrine, I tell you, is true," said the lama, raising

his arms and assuming a remarkable accent of authority. "It is the doctrine of the west, but it is of unfathomable profundity. It cannot be sounded to the bottom."

These words of the Tibetan lama astonished us greatly: the Unity of God, the mystery of the Incarnation, the dogma of the Real Presence, seemed to us enveloped in his creed. Yet with ideas so apparently sound, he accepted also the doctrine of transmigration, and a sort of pantheism of which he could give no account. These new revelations respecting the religion of Buddha gave us hopes that we should really find among the lamas of Tibet a symbolism more refined than, and superior to, the common belief, and confirmed us in the resolution we had adopted, of keeping on our course westward.

Before quitting the inn, we called in the landlord to settle our bill. We had calculated that the board and lodging of three men and our animals for four days would cost us at least two ounces of silver. We were therefore agreeably surprised to hear the landlord say: "Sirs Lamas, there is no occasion for going into any accounts: put three hundred sapeks into the till, and that will do very well. My house," he added, "is recently established, and I want to give it a good character. You are come from a distant land, and I wish to enable you to say to your countrymen that my establishment is worthy of their confidence."

We replied that we would everywhere mention his disinterestedness; and that our countrymen, whenever they had occasion to visit Blue Town, would certainly not fail to put up at the Hotel of the Three Perfections.

We quitted Blue Town on the fourth day of the ninth moon. We had already been traveling more than a month. It was with the utmost difficulty that our little caravan could get out of the town: the streets were encumbered with men, carts, animals, stalls in which the traders displayed their goods. We could advance only step by step, and at times we were obliged to come to a halt and wait for some minutes until the way became a little cleared. It was near noon before we reached the last houses of the town, outside the western gate. There, upon a level road, our camels were at length able to proceed at their ease in all the fulness of their long step. A chain of rugged rocks rising on our right sheltered us so completely from the north wind that we did not at all feel the rigor of the weather. The country through which we were now traveling was still a portion of Western Toumet.

10

Crossing the Yellow River

WE had been quite prepared to pass the Yellow River under circumstances of danger arising from the wretchedness of the ferryboats and the difficulty of managing our camels in them. We knew, too, of course, that the Hwang-Ho was subject to periodical overflows. We proceeded forthwith towards the river to investigate the matter for ourselves. We found that the Yellow River had become, as it were, a vast sea, the limits of which were scarcely visible. Here and there we could see the higher grounds rising above the water, like islands, while the houses and villages looked as though they were floating upon the waves. We consulted several persons as to the course to adopt. Some said that further progress was impracticable, because, even where the inundation had subsided, it had left the earth so soft and slippery that the camels could not walk upon it; while elsewhere we should have to dread at every step some deep pool, in which we should inevitably be drowned. Other opinions were more favorable, suggesting that the boats which were stationed at intervals for the purpose would easily and cheaply convey us and our baggage in three days to the river, while the camels could follow us through the water, and that at the river side the great ferryboat would carry us over the bed of the stream without difficulty.

What were we to do? To turn back was out of the question. We had vowed that, God aiding, we would go to

Lhasa, no matter what obstacles might be encountered. Following the river northwards would materially augment the length of our journey, and, moreover, compel us to traverse the great desert of Gobi. To remain at an inn, and patiently await for a month the complete subsiding of the waters and the restoration of solidity in the roads was, from one point of view, the most prudent course, but there was a grave inconvenience about it. We and our five animals could not live for a month in an inn without occasioning a most alarming atrophy in our already meager purse. The only course remaining was to place ourselves exclusively under the protection of Divine Providence, and to go on, regardless of mud or marsh.

So that is what we did, and we were soon up to the knees of the camels in a thick, slimy compost of mud and water, covering other somewhat firmer mud. Through this the poor animals slowly slid on their painful way, their heads turning alternately right and left, their limbs trembling, and the sweat exuding from each pore. Every moment we expected them to fall beneath us. It was near noon ere we arrived at a little village. There a few wretched people, whose rags scarce covered their gaunt frames, gathered around and accompanied us to the edge of a broad piece of water, a portion of a lake. This, they told us we must cross, and some boatmen among them proposed to carry us over this lake to the dike.

The embarkation was effected with extraordinary celerity, and we soon quitted the shore. Whilst we advanced by being rowed on the surface of the lake, a man mounted on a camel, and leading two others after him, entered the lake. He followed a course traced out by a small boat rowed by another man. The latter was obliged every now and then to sound the depth of the water, and the camel driver needed to be very attentive in directing his course in the straight trail left by the boat, lest he should be swallowed up in the holes beneath the water. The camels advanced slowly, stretching out their long necks, and at times leaving only their heads and part of their humps visible above the lake. We were in continual alarm; for these animals were not able to swim, and only one false step was needed to precipitate any of them to the bottom. Thanks to the protection of God, all arrived safely at the dike which had been pointed out to us.

The boatmen, after assisting us to replace our baggage on the camels, indicated the point whither we must direct our steps: "Do you see, to the right, that small temple? A little from the temple, do you observe those wooden huts and those black nets hanging from long poles? There you will find the ferryboat to cross the river. Follow this dike, and go in peace."

After having proceeded with difficulty for half an hour, we reached the ferryboat. The boatmen immediately came to us. "Sirs Lamas," said they, "you intend, doubtless, to cross the Hwang-Ho, but you see this evening the thing is impracticable—the sun is just setting."

"You are right; we will cross tomorrow at daybreak. Meanwhile, let us settle the price, so that tomorrow we may lose no time in deliberation."

The boatman would have preferred waiting till the morrow to discuss this important point, expecting we should offer a much larger sum when just about to embark. At first their demands were preposterous: but happily, there were two boats which competed together, for otherwise we should have been ruined. The price was ultimately fixed at one thousand sapeks. The passage was not long, it is true, for the river had nearly resumed its bed; but the waters were very rapid, and, moreover, the camels had to ride. The amount, enormous in itself, appeared, upon the whole, moderate, considering the difficulty and trouble of the passage.

This business arranged, we considered how we should pass the night. We looked for a place whereon to set up our tent; but we could find nowhere a spot sufficiently dry: mud or stagnant water covered the ground in all directions. About a hundred yards from the shore was a small temple of idols. A narrow, high path led to it, and we proceeded thither to see if we could find a place of repose. A portico, supported by three stone pillars, stood before the entrance door, which was secured by a large padlock. This portico, made of granite, was raised a few feet from the ground, and was reached by five steps. We determined to pass the night there.

Samdadchiemba asked if it would not be a monstrous superstition to sleep on the steps of a temple. When we had relieved his scruples, he made sundry philosophical reflections. "Behold," said he, "a temple which has been built by the people of the country, in honor of the god of the river. Yet, when it rained in Tibet, the idol had no power to preserve itself from the flood. Nevertheless, this temple serves at present to shelter two missioners of God—the only real use it has ever served!" So our Dchiahour, who at first had scrupled to lodge under the portico of this idolatrous temple, now thought the idea magnificent, and laughed heartily.

After having arranged our luggage in this singular encampment, we proceeded to say our rosaries on the shores of the Hwang-Ho. The moon was brilliant and lit up this immense river, which rolled its yellow and tumultuous waters over a smooth bed. The Hwang-Ho is beyond doubt one of the finest rivers in the world. It rises in the mountains of Tibet, and crosses the Koko-nor, entering China by Kansu Province. Thence it follows the sandy regions at the foot of the Ala-Shan Mountains, encircles the country of Ordos; and, after having watered China first from north to south, and then from west to east, it falls into the Yellow Sea. The waters of the Hwang-Ho, pure and clear at their source, take the yellow hue only after having passed the sands of the Ala-Shan and Ordos. They are almost continuously level with the lands through which they flow, and it is this circumstance that occasions those inundations so disastrous to the Chinese. As for the Tartar nomads, when the waters rise, all they have to do is to strike their tents and drive their herds elsewhere.

Though the Yellow River had cost us so much trouble, we derived much satisfaction from taking a walk at night upon its solitary banks, and listening to the solemn murmur of its majestic waters. We were contemplating this grand work of nature, when Samdadchiemba recalled us to the prose of life by announcing that the oatmeal was ready. Our repast was as brief as it was plain. We then stretched ourselves on our goatskins, in the portico, so that we three described the three sides of a triangle, in the center of which we piled our baggage; for we had no faith at all that the sanctity of the place would deter robbers, if robbers were in the vicinity.

As we have mentioned, the little temple was dedicated to the divinity of the Yellow River. The idol, seated on a pedestal of gray brick, was hideous, as are all those idols that one ordinarily sees in Chinese pagodas. From a broad, flat, red face, rose two great staring eyes, like eggs stuck into orbits, the smaller ends projecting. Thick eyebrows, instead of describing a horizontal line, began at the bottom of each ear and met in the middle of the forehead, so as to form an obtuse angle. The idol had on its head a seashell, and brandished, with a menacing air, a sword like a scythe. This idol had, at right and at left, two attendants, who were putting out their tongues and apparently making faces at it.

Just as we were lying down, a man approached us, holding in one hand a small paper lantern. He opened the grating which led to the interior of the temple, prostrated himself thrice, burned incense in the censers, and lighted a small lamp at the feet of the idol. This personage was not a bonze. His hair, hanging in a braid, and his blue garments, showed him to be a layman. When he had finished his idolatrous ceremonies, he came to us. "I will leave the door open," said he. "You'll sleep more comfortably inside than in the portico."

"Thanks," replied we. "Shut the door, however; for we shall do very well where we are. Why have you been burning incense? Who is the idol of this place?"

"It is the spirit of the Hwang-Ho, who inhabits this temple. I have burned incense before him, in order that our fishing may be productive and that our boats may float without danger."

"The words you utter," cried Samdadchiemba, insolently, "are mere stuff and nonsense! How did it happen that the other day, when the inundation took place, the temple was flooded and your idol was covered with mud?" To this sudden apostrophe the pagan churchwarden made no answer, but he took to his heels. We were much surprised at this proceeding; but the explanation came next morning.

We stretched ourselves on our goatskins once more, and endeavored to sleep, but sleep came slowly and for but a brief period. Situated between marshes and the river, we felt throughout the night a piercing cold, which seemed to transfix us to the very marrow. The sky was clear and serene, and in the morning we saw that the marshes were covered with a thick sheet of ice. We began preparations for departure.

Upon collecting our various articles, we learned that a handkerchief was missing. We remembered that we had imprudently hung it upon the grating at the entrance of the temple, so that it was half in and half out of the building. No person had been near the place, except the man who had come to pay his devotions to the idol. We could, therefore, without much rashness, attribute the robbery to him, and this explained why he had made his departure so rapidly, without replying to Samdadchiemba. It would have been easy to catch the thief, but to do so would have been to stir up trouble for nothing.

We placed our baggage upon the camels and proceeded to the riverside, fully persuaded that we had a miserable day before us. Camels have a horror of the water, and therefore it is sometimes impossible to make them get into a boat. The driver may pull their noses, or nearly kill them with blows, yet not succeed in making them advance a step; they would rather die. The boat before us seemed to present almost insurmountable obstacles. It was not flat and large, like those which generally serve as ferryboats: its sides were very high, so that the animals were obliged to leap over them at the risk and peril of breaking their legs. If one wished to move a carriage into it, the vehicle had to be taken apart.

The boatmen had already started to lift our baggage, for the purpose of conveying it into their abominable vessel, but we stopped them. "Wait a moment; we must first try and get the camels in. If they won't enter the boat, there is no use in placing the baggage in it."

"Whence came your camels, that they can't get into people's boats?"

"It matters little whence they came. What we tell you is that the tall white camel has never hitherto consented to cross any river, even in a flat boat."

"Tall camel or short, flat boat or high boat, into the boat the camel shall go!" And so saying, the ferryman ran and fetched an immense cudgel. "Catch hold of the string in the camel's nose!" cried he to a companion. "We'll see if we can't make the beast get into the boat."

The man in the boat hauled at the string, the man behind beat the animal vehemently on the legs with his cudgel, but all to no purpose. The poor camel sent forth piercing cries, and stretched out its long neck. Blood flowed from its nostrils; sweat flowed from every pore; but not an inch would the creature move. Yet one step would have placed it in the boat, the sides of which were touched by its forelegs. We could not endure the painful spectacle. "No

more of this!" we cried to the ferryman. "It is useless to
beat the animal. You might break its legs or kill it before
it would consent to enter your boat."

The two men at once left off, for they were tired, the
one of pulling, the other of beating. But what were we to
do? We had almost made up our minds to ascend the banks
of the river to find some flat boat, when the ferryman all
at once jumped up, radiant with an idea. "We will make
another attempt," cried he, "and if that fails I give the
matter up. Take the string gently," he added to a companion, "and keep the camel's feet as close as ever you can
to the side of the boat."

Then, going back for some paces, he dashed forward with
a spring and threw himself with all his weight upon the animal's rear. The shock, so violent and unexpected, caused
the camel to bend its forelegs. A second shock immediately
succeeded the first, and the animal, in order to prevent itself from falling into the water, had no choice but to raise
its feet and place them within the boat. This effected, the
rest was easy. A few pinches of the nose and a few blows
sufficed to impel the hind legs after the fore—and the white
camel was at last in the boat, to the extreme satisfaction of
all present. The other animals were embarked after the
same fashion, and we proceeded on our watery way.

11
Mud and Pilgrims

AFTER a long, laborious, dangerous passage, we reached the other side of the waters. Samdadchiemba had arrived long before us, and was awaiting us on the margin of the stream. He was naked as to clothes, but was covered well nigh to the shoulders with a thick layer of mud, which gave him a Negro aspect. In consequence of the extreme shallowness of the water, the boat could not get within thirty feet of the shore. The boatmen who preceded us had been obliged to carry passengers on their shoulders from the boats. We did not choose to adopt the same process, but rather to make use of the animals for our disembarkation. Samdadchiemba accordingly brought them close to the boat; Father Gabet got on the horse, Father Huc on the mule; and so we reached the shore, without having occasion to employ human carriers.

The sun was about to set. We would willingly have encamped at once, for we were exhausted with hunger and fatigue, but we could not possibly do so, for we had, they told us, fully two li to journey before we should get out of the mud. We loaded our camels, therefore, and proceeded onward, completing the miserable day in pain and suffering. Night closed in before we came to a place where we could set up our tent; we had no strength left for preparing the usual meal, so, drinking some cold water and eating a few handfuls of millet, we lay down, after a brief prayer, and fell into a deep slumber.

The sun was already very high when we rose. On leaving the tent we looked around us, in order to get acquainted with this new country, which the darkness of the preceding evening had not allowed us to examine. It appeared to us dismal and arid; but we were happy, on any terms, to lose sight of bogs and swamps. We had left behind us the Yellow River, with its overflowing waters, and entered the sandy steppes of Ordos.

On the fifteenth day of the new moon, we came upon numerous caravans following, like ourselves, the direction from east to west. The road was filled with men, women, and children, riding on camels or oxen. They were all repairing, they said, to the lamasery of Rashe-Chruin. When they had asked whether our journey had the same object, they were surprised at receiving an answer in the negative. The number of these pilgrims, and the astonishment they showed upon hearing that we were not going to the lamasery of Rashe-Chruin, excited our curiosity.

At the turn of a ravine, we overtook an old lama, who, laden with a heavy pack, seemed to make his way with great labor and pain. "Brother," said we, "you are old; your black hairs are not so numerous as the gray. Doubtless your fatigue must be extreme. Place your burden upon one of our camels; that will relieve you a little."

Upon hearing these words the old man prostrated himself before us in order to express his gratitude. We made a camel kneel, and Samdadchiemba added to our baggage that of the lama. As soon as the pilgrim was relieved of the weight which had oppressed him, his walk became more elastic, and an expression of satisfaction was diffused over his countenance. "Brother," said we, "we are from the west, and the affairs of your country are not well known to us. We are astonished at finding so many pilgrims here in the desert."

"We are all going to Rashe-Chruin," replied he, in accents full of emotion.

"Doubtless," said we, "some grand solemnity calls you together?"

"Yes, tomorrow will be a great day. A lama *Botké* will manifest his power: kill himself, yet not die." We at once understood what solemnity it was that thus attracted the Ortous Tartars. A lama was to cut himself open, take out his entrails and place them before him, and eventually restore them and resume his previous condition.

This spectacle, so cruel and disgusting, is very common in the lamaseries of Tartary. The *Botké* who is to manifest his power, as the Mongols phrase it, prepares himself for the formidable operation by many days of fasting and prayer, during which he must abstain from all communication whatever with mankind and observe the most absolute silence. When the appointed day is come, the multitude of pilgrims assemble in the great court of the lamasery, where an altar is raised in front of the temple gate. At length the *Botké* appears. He advances gravely, amid the acclamations of the crowd, seats himself upon the altar, and takes from his girdle a large knife which he places upon his knees. At his feet, numerous lamas, ranged in a circle, commence the terrible invocations of this frightful ceremony.

As the recitation of the prayers proceeds, the *Botké* trembles in every limb, and gradually works himself into frenzied convulsions. The lamas themselves become excited: their voices are raised; their song observes no order, and at last becomes a mere confusion of yelling and outcry. Then the *Botké* suddenly throws aside the scarf which envelopes him, unfastens his girdle, and, seizing the sacred knife, slits open his stomach, in one long cut. While the blood flows in every direction, the multitude prostrate themselves before the terrible spectacle, and the enthusiast is interrogated about all sorts of hidden things, such as future events, the destiny of certain personages, and so forth. The replies of the *Botké* to all these questions are regarded by everybody as oracles.

When the devout curiosity of the numerous pilgrims has been satisfied, the lamas resume, but now calmly and gravely, the recitation of their prayers. The *Botké* takes, in his right hand, blood from his wound, raises it to his mouth, breathes thrice upon it, and then throws it into the air with loud cries. He next restores the entrails, passes his hand rapidly over his wound, closes it—and soon everything resumes its original condition. No trace remains of the diabolical operation, except extreme prostration. The *Bokté* once more rolls his scarf round him, and recites in a low voice a short prayer; then all is over, and the multitude disperse, with the exception of a few of the especially devout, who remain to contemplate and to adore the bloodstained altar which the "saint" has quitted.

These horrible ceremonies are of frequent occurrence in the great lamaseries of Tartary and Tibet, and we do not believe that there is any trick or deception about them; for, from all we have seen and heard among idolatrous nations, we are persuaded that the devil has a great deal to do with the matter. Moreover, our impression that there is no trick in the operation is fortified by the opinion of the most intelligent and most upright Buddhists whom we have met in the numerous lamaseries we visited.

12

Salt and Camels

AT a short distance from Rashe-Churin, we reached a road well marked out and covered with travelers. It was not, however, devotion that had set them in motion, as had been the case with the pilgrims whom we saw at the lamasery. A matter of business was leading these people towards the Dabsun nor, for it is a salt lake, celebrated throughout Western Manchu, and it supplies with salt not only the adjacent Tartars, but also several provinces of the Chinese Empire.

For a day's journey before the traveler reaches Dabsun nor, the soil changes by degrees its form and aspect: losing its yellow tint, it gradually becomes white, as though thinly covered with snow. The earth, swelling in every direction, forms innumerable hillocks, cone-shaped, and of a regularity so perfect that one might suppose them to have been constructed by the hand of man. Sometimes they are grouped in heaps, one on the other. They are of all sizes, some but just created, others old and falling to decay. Around these mounds grow creeping thorns, long-pointed, without flowers or leaves, which, intertwining spirally, surmount them with a sort of network cap. These thorns are never found elsewhere than about these hillocks: upon those of more recent growth they are firm, vigorous, and full of shoots; upon the elder elevations they are dried up, calcined by niter, brittle, and in shreds.

As one looks upon these numerous mounds, covered with

a thick efflorescence of niter, it is obvious that beneath the surface, and at no great depth, some great chemical operation is in progress. Springs, generally so rare in the Ordos country, are here of frequent occurrence, but the water is for the most part excessively salty. Here and there, however, by the very side of a brackish pool, there is a spring of soft, sweet, delicious water; all such springs are indicated to travelers by a small flag, fluttering from the end of a long pole.

Dabsun nor is not so much a lake as a reservoir of mineral salt, mixed with nitrous efflorescence. The latter, in color white, and crumbling between the fingers, is easily distinguishable from the salt, which is of a gray tint and glitters like crystal when broken. Dabsun nor is about twenty li in circumference. Around it, at intervals, are the tents occupied by the Mongols who work it, and the Chinese who have thrust themselves in as partners. It would be difficult indeed to find any variety of industry or commerce, within a certain range of their own country, in which the Chinese do not contrive to have a hand.

The manipulation to which the salt is subjected requires neither great labor nor great science. All the workers do is to pick it up as it is found in the reservoir; to pile it; and, when the heap is of a certain size, to cover it with a thin coating of potter's earth. When the salt has sufficiently purified itself, the Tartars convey it to the nearest Chinese mart and exchange it for tea, tobacco, brandy, and other commodities. In the locality itself, salt is of no value: at every step one sees lumps of it, sometimes of remarkable purity. We filled a bag with these for our own use and for that of the camels, which are all very fond of salt.

We traversed Dabsun nor throughout its breadth from east to west, and we had to take the utmost precaution as we proceeded over its loose, and at times almost moving, soil. The Tartars advised us not to deviate in the least from the path we should find marked out, and by all means to

avoid any places where we should see the water bubbling
up, for there, they informed us, were depths which they had
frequently endeavored to sound, but without result. This
statement induced us to believe that there is a *nor*, or lake,
here, but that it is underground, the place called Dabsun
nor being merely the covering or roof of the lake, composed
of the saline and nitrous matter produced by the constant
evaporation of the subterranean waters. Foreign matter,
brought by the wind and consolidated by the rain, would
in the lapse of time form a crust upon such a roof, strong
enough to bear the caravans that incessantly traverse
Dabsun nor.

This great salt mine seems to pervade with its influence
the whole Ordos district, throughout the extent of which
the water is brackish, the soil arid, and the surface encrusted with saline matter. This absence of rich pasturage
and fresh water is very unfavorable for the raising of cattle;
but the camel, whose robust and hardy temperament adapts
itself to the most sterile regions, affords compensation to
the Tartars of Ordos. This animal, a perfect treasure to the
dwellers in the desert, can remain a fortnight, or even a
month, without eating or drinking. However wretched the
land may be on which it is put to feed, it can always find
something wherewith to satisfy its hunger, especially if the
soil be impregnated with salt or niter. Things that no
other animal will touch, to it are welcome: briers and
thorns, dry wood itself, supply it with nourishing food.

Though it costs so little to keep, the camel is useful to a
degree inconceivable to those who are not acquainted with
the countries in which Providence has placed it. The camel's
ordinary load is from seven hundred to eight hundred
pounds, and the animal can carry this load ten leagues a
day. Those camels which are employed to carry despatches
are expected to travel eighty leagues a day, but then they
carry only the despatch bearer. In several countries of
Tartary, the carriages of kings and princes are drawn by

camels, and sometimes these animals are harnessed to palanquins; but this can only be done in the level country. The fleshy nature of the camel's feet does not permit them to climb mountains when they have a carriage or litter of any sort to draw after them.

The training of the young camel is a business requiring great care and attention. For the first week of its life, it can neither stand nor suck without some helping hand. Its long neck is then of such excessive flexibility and fragility that it runs the risk of dislocating it. The camel, born to servitude, seems impressed from its birth with a sense of the yoke it is destined to bear through life. One never sees the young camel playing and frolicking about, as one sees kids, colts, and other young animals. It is always grave, melancholy, and slow in its movements; it never hastens, unless under compulsion. In the night, and often in the day also, it sends forth a mournful cry, like that of an infant in pain. It seems to feel that joy or recreation is not within its portion; that its inevitable career is forced labor and long fastings, until death shall relieve it.

The maturing of the camel is a long affair. A camel cannot carry even a single rider until its third year; and it is not in full vigor until it is eight years old. Its trainers then begin to try it with loads, which are gradually made heavier and heavier. When the camel can rise with its burden, this is a proof that it can carry it throughout the journey. When that journey is only of brief duration, the driver sometimes loads the animal in excess, and then aids it to rise by means of bars or levers. The camel's capacity for labor endures for a long time. Provided that at certain periods of the year it is allowed a short holiday for pasturing at its leisure, it will continue its service for fully fifty years.

Nature has provided the camel with no means of defense against other animals, unless one may so consider its piercing, prolonged cry, and its huge, shapeless, ugly frame, which at a distance resembles a heap of ruins. The camel seldom kicks, and, when it does, it almost as seldom inflicts any injury. Its soft, fleshy foot cannot wound, or even bruise; neither can the camel bite an antagonist. In fact, its only practical means of defense against man or beast is a sort of vehement sneeze, by which it discharges, from nose and mouth, a mass of filth against the object which it seeks to intimidate or to annoy.

When about to take repose, the camel kneels down, folds its forelegs symmetrically under its body, and stretches out its long neck before it on the ground. In this position it looks just like a monstrous snail.

The awkward aspect of the camel, the excessive stench of its breath, its heavy, ungraceful movements, its projecting harelips, the callosities which disfigure various parts of its body, all contribute to render its appearance repulsive; yet its extreme gentleness and docility, and its services to man, render it of preeminent utility, and make us forget its deformity.

Every year, towards the close of spring, the camel sheds its hair, every individual bristle of which disappears before a single sprout of the new stock comes up. For twenty days the animal remains completely bare, as though it had been closely shaved all over, from the top of the head to the extremity of the tail. At this period, it is excessively sensitive to cold or wet; and one sees it, at the slightest chilliness in the air or the least drop of rain, shivering and shaking in every limb, like a naked man exposed on the snow. By degrees the new hair shows itself, in the form of fine, soft, curling wool, which gradually becomes a long, thick fur, capable of resisting the extremest inclemency of the weather. Then the greatest delight of the animal is to walk in the teeth of the north wind, or to stand motionless on the summit of a hill, beaten by the storm and inhaling the icy wind. Some naturalists say that the camel cannot exist in cold countries; these writers must have wholly forgotten the Tartarian camels, which, on the contrary, cannot endure the least heat and which certainly could not exist in Arabia.

The hair of an ordinary camel weighs about ten pounds. It is sometimes finer than silk, and always longer than sheep's wool. The hair growing below the neck and on the legs of the Tartar camels is rough, bushy, and in color black; whereas that of the ordinary camel is red, gray, and white. In the places where the animals pasture, great sheets of their hair, looking like dirty rags, are driven about by the wind until they are accumulated in sheltered corners near the hillsides. The utmost use the Tartars make of the hair is to twist some of it into cord, or into a sort of canvas, of which they construct sacks and carpets.

The milk of the camel is excellent, and supplies large quantities of butter and cheese. The flesh is hard, unsavory, and little esteemed by the Tartars. They use the hump however: this, cut into slices and dissolved in tea, serves the purpose of butter.

13

Mongol Friend

THE environs of the Dabsun nor abound in flocks of goats and sheep. These animals like to browse on the furze and thorny bushes, the sole vegetation of these barren steppes; they especially delight in those nitrous efflorescences which are found here in the utmost abundance. The soil, miserable though it is in other respects, seems very favorable to the growth of these animals, which enter largely into the economy of the Tartars, constituting indeed the basis of their food. If bought on the spot, sheep and goats are of very moderate price. As we calculated that a pound of meat would cost us less than a pound of flour, we resolved to buy a sheep. The thing was not difficult to find; but as it would of course oblige us to stop, at least for a day, we waited till we should come to some place not quite barren, where our animals could find some pasturage to browse upon.

Two days after crossing Dabsun nor, we entered a long narrow valley, where some Mongol families had stationed themselves. The earth was close by covered with an herb which, in form and character, had much resemblance to thyme. Our beasts, as they proceeded, browsed furtively, right and left, on this plant, and seemed to be very fond of it. This new pasturage gave us the idea of encamping on the spot. Not far from a tent, a lama was sitting on a hillock, making ropes with camel's hair. "Brother," said we as we approached him, "the flock upon the hill doubtless belongs to you. Will you sell us a sheep?"

"Certainly," he answered, "I will let you have an excellent sheep. As to the price, we will not quarrel about that: we men of prayer are not like merchants." He indicated to us a spot near his own tent, and unloaded our beasts. The entire family of the lama, when they heard the cries of our camels, hastened to assist us to encamp. We, indeed, were not allowed to do anything; for our new friends took delight in making themselves useful, in unsaddling the beasts, pitching the tent, and putting our baggage in order within.

The young lama who had received us with so much kindness, after having unsaddled the horse and the mule, perceived that both these beasts were hurt a little on the back. "Brothers," he said, "here is a bad business; and, as you are upon a long journey, it must be remedied, or you will not be able to go on."

So saying, he took the knife which hung from his girdle, sharpened it with rapidity upon his boot tops, took our saddles to pieces, examined the rough parts of the wood, and pared them away on both sides till he had removed the slightest unevenness. He then put together again, with wonderful skill, all the pieces of the saddles, and returned them to us. "That will do," said he. "Now you may travel in peace."

This operation was effected rapidly and in the readiest manner possible. The lama was then about to fetch the sheep; but, as it was already late, we said it was unnecessary, for we should remain a whole day in his valley.

Next morning, before we were awake, the lama opened the door of our tent, laughing so loud that he aroused us. "Ah," said he, "I see plainly that you do not intend to depart today. The sun is already very high, and you sleep still."

We rose quickly. As soon as we were dressed, the lama

spoke of the sheep. "Come to the flock," he said; "you may choose at your pleasure."

"No, go by yourself and select a sheep for us. At present we have an occupation. With us, lamas of the western sky, it is a rule to pray as soon as we rise."

"Oh, what a fine thing!" said the lama; "oh, the holy rules of the west!" His admiration, however, did not make him forget his little affair of business. He mounted his horse and rode towards a flock of sheep which we saw undulating upon the slope of a hill.

We had not yet finished our prayers when we heard the Tartar returning at full gallop. He had fastened the sheep to the back of his saddle, like a portmanteau. Hardly arrived at the door of our tent, he dismounted; and in the twinkling of an eye he had put upon its four legs the poor sheep, quite astounded at the ride it had been favored with.

"That is the sheep. Is it not fine? Does it suit you?"

Considering the size of the animal, we thought the price moderate. "You ask an ounce. Here is an ingot, which is just of the weight you require. Sit down for a moment; we will fetch our scales, and you shall ascertain whether this piece of silver really weighs an ounce."

At these words the lama drew back, and cried, stretching out both hands towards us: "Above there is a heaven, below there is the earth, and Buddha is the lord of all things. He wills that men behave towards each other like brothers. You are of the west, I am of the east. Is that any reason why the intercourse between us should not be frank and honorable? You have not belittled my sheep: I take your money without weighing it."

"An excellent principle," said we. "As you will not weigh the money, pray sit, nevertheless, for a moment; we will take a cup of tea together and talk over a little matter."

"1 know what you mean: neither you nor I may cause the transmigration of this living being. We must find a lay-man who knows how to kill sheep. Is it not so?" And with-

out awaiting an answer, he added, "Another thing: from
your appearance, one may easily guess that you are no great
hands at cutting up sheep and preparing them."

"You are not mistaken," we answered, laughing.

"Well, keep the sheep tied to your tent; and for the rest,
rely upon me. I shall be back in a minute." He mounted
his horse, went off at full gallop, and disappeared in a bend
of the vale.

The lama soon returned. He tied his horse to a post, took
off his saddle, bridle, and halter, gave the horse a cut with
his whip, and so sent it off to pasture. He went into his
tent for a little while, and then appeared with all the members of his family; that is to say, his old mother and two
younger brothers. They advanced slowly towards our tent,
in truly ridiculous fashion, just as if they were going to
transfer all their furniture. The lama carried on his head
a large pot, which covered him as with an enormous hat.
His mother had on her back a large basket, filled with
argols. The two young Mongols followed with a trivet, an
iron spoon, and several other minor kitchen implements.
At this sight Samdadchiemba was full of joy, for he saw
before him a whole day of poetry.

When the entire culinary department was arranged in
the open air, the lama, in his politeness, invited us to go
and repose in our tent awhile. He judged from our air that
we could not, without loss of class, be present at the approaching scene of butchering. The suggestion, however,
did not meet our views, and we requested that, if we could
do so without inconveniencing the family, we might sit
down on the grass at a respectful distance, with the promise
that we would touch nothing. After some objections, perceiving that we were curious to be spectators, the Mongols
dispensed with the etiquette of the occasion.

The lama seemed anxious; he kept looking towards the
north of the valley, as if expecting some one. "All right,"
he said at last, with an air of satisfaction; "here he comes."

"Who comes? Of whom do you speak?"

"I forgot to tell you that I had been just now to invite a layman to come, one who is very skillful in killing a sheep. There he is."

We rose and perceived, indeed, something moving among the verdure of the valley. At first we could not clearly distinguish what it was, for, though it advanced with some rapidity, the object did not seem to enlarge. At last the most singular person we had ever met in our lives presented himself to our view. We were obliged to make the utmost efforts to repress an exclamation of amazement. This layman seemed to be about fifty years old, but his height did not exceed three feet. On the top of his head, which terminated like a sugar loaf, rose a small tuft of badly combed hair; a gray, thin beard descended in disorder down his chin. Finally, two humps, one on his back, the other on his breast, gave to this little butcher a perfect resemblance to Aesop, as the latter appears in various editions of the *Fables*.

The strong, sonorous voice of the layman was in singular contrast with his thin, stunted frame. He did not lose much time in saluting the company. After darting his small black eyes at the sheep, which was tied to one of the nails of our tent, he said: "Is this the beast you wish to have put in order?" And, while feeling its tail in order to judge its fat, he gave it a turn, and placed it on its back with remarkable dexterity. He next tied together its legs; then, while uncovering his right arm by throwing back the sleeve of his leather coat, he asked whether the operation was to be effected in the tent or outside.

"Outside," said we.

"Outside; very well, outside." So saying, he drew from a leather sheath, suspended from his sash, a knife with a large handle, the blade of which had by long use become thin and narrow. After having examined for a moment its point with his thumb, he plunged it to the hilt into the side of the sheep; then drew it out quite red. The sheep was dead,

dead at once, without making any movement. Not a single drop of blood had spouted from the wound. We were greatly astonished at this, and asked the little man how he managed to kill a sheep so very easily and quickly.

"We Tartars," he said, "do not kill in the same way as the Chinese. They cut the throat; we go straight to the heart. By our method the animal suffers less, and all the blood is, as it should be, retained in the interior."

The "transmigration" once accomplished, nobody had any further scruples. Our Dchiahour and the Tartar lama turned back their sleeves and advanced to assist the little butcher. The sheep was skinned with admirable celerity. Meantime the mother of the lama had made the two pots boil. She took the entrails of the sheep, washed them pretty clean, and then, with the blood which she took from the interior of the sheep by means of a large wooden spoon, prepared some puddings, the basis of which was the never-failing oatmeal.

"Sirs Lamas," said the little layman, "shall I bone the sheep?" Upon our answering in the affirmative, he had the animal hooked upon the tent, for he was not big enough to perform that operation himself. Then he mounted upon a large stone, and, passing his knife rapidly along the bones, detached, in one piece, all the meat, so as to leave dangling from the tent a mere skeleton, clean, cleared, and nicely polished.

14

The Feast

WHILE the little layman was, according to his expression, putting in order the flesh of the sheep, the rest of the company had prepared a celebration in the Tartar fashion. The young lama was director of the feast. "Now," he cried, "let us all sit around; the great pot is going to be emptied!"

Forthwith everyone sat down upon the turf. The old Mongol woman plunged both hands into the pot, which was boiling over, and drew out the liver, the heart, the kidneys, the spleen, and the bowels, stuffed with blood and oatmeal. In this gastronomical preparation, the most remarkable thing was that all the organs had been retained in their integrity, so that they appeared much as they are seen in the living beast. The old woman served up, or rather threw, this splendid dish upon the lawn, which was at once our chair, table, plate, and, in case of need, our napkin. It is unnecessary to add that we used our fingers instead of forks. Everyone seized with his hands a portion of the viscera, twisted it from the mass, and devoured it without seasoning or salt.

The two missioners were not able, despite their utmost willingness, to do honor to this Tartar dish. First we burned our fingers when we tried to touch the hot and smoking repast. Although our guests insisted that it ought not to be allowed to grow cold, we waited a little, afraid of burning our lips also. At last we tasted these puddings of sheep's blood and oatmeal; but after getting down a few mouthfuls, we were quite satisfied. Never, perhaps, had we eaten anything so utterly tasteless and insipid. Samdadchiemba, having foreseen this, had withdrawn from the common dish the liver and the kidneys; these he placed before us, with some salt, which he had previously crushed between two stones. We were thus enabled to keep pace with the company, who, with a devouring appetite, were swallowing the vast system of entrails.

When the whole had disappeared, the old woman brought on the second service, by placing in the midst of us the large pot in which the puddings had been cooked. Instantly all the members of the banquet invited each other, and, everyone taking from his bosom his wooden porringer, ladled out bumpers of a smoking, salt liquid, which they dignified with the pompous name of gravy. As we did not wish to appear eccentric, or as if we despised the Tartar cuisine, we acted like the rest. We plunged our porringer into the pot, but it was only by the most laudable efforts that we could down this green stuff, which gave us the impression of being half-masticated grass. The Tartars, on the contrary, found it delicious, and readily reached the bottom of the extempore tureen, not stopping for a moment, till nothing was left—not a drop of gravy, not an inch of pudding.

When the feast was finished, the little layman took leave, receiving as his fee the four feet of the sheep. To this fee, fixed by the old custom of the Mongols, we added, as a supplement, a handful of tea leaves, for we desired that he should long remember and talk to his countrymen of the generosity of the lamas of the western sky.

Every one having been thoroughly regaled, our neighbors took their kitchen utensils and returned home, except the young lama, who said he would not leave us alone. After much talk about the east and west, he took down the skeleton, which was still hanging at the entrance of the tent, and amused himself with reciting, or rather singing, the names of all the bones, large and small, that compose the frame of the sheep. He perceived that our knowledge on this subject was very limited, and this astonished him: we had the greatest trouble to make him understand that in our country ecclesiastical studies have for their object more serious and important matters than the names and number of the bones of a sheep.

Every Mongol knows the number, the names, and the position of the bones which compose the frame of animals; and thus they never break the bones when they are cutting up an ox or a sheep. With the point of their large knife, they go straight and at once to the junctures of the bones and separate them with astonishing skill and celerity. These frequent dissections, added to the habit of being every day amongst their flocks, make the Tartars well acquainted with the diseases of animals and skillful in their cure. The remedies, which they employ internally, are always herbs gathered in the prairie and made into a decoction which they give the sick animals to drink. For administering the medicine, the Tartars use a large cow horn. When they have contrived to insert the small end of this into the mouth of the animal, they pour the physic in at the other extremity, as through a funnel. If the beast persists in not opening its mouth, the liquid is administered through the nostrils.

The young lama who had sold us the sheep spent a great part of the day in telling us anecdotes, more or less piquant and curious, about veterinary science, in which he seemed to be very skillful. Moreover, he gave us important instructions concerning the road we were to pursue. He settled the stages we ought to make, and indicated the places where we should encamp so as to prevent our dying from thirst.

After two days' journey we reached the foot of a chain of mountains, the summits of which were lost in the clouds. We set about ascending them courageously. That day's journey was very painful, especially to the camels, for every step was upon sharp, rugged rock; and the animals' feet, accordingly, were very speedily bleeding. We ourselves were too absorbed with the strange, fantastic aspect of the mountains we were traversing to think of the toil they occasioned us. It was near noon when we reached the crest of these mountains, and we hoped to sleep at night in the little town of Shih-Tsui-Tzu, which we perceived on the slope of a hill before us.

We occupied the whole afternoon in descending the rugged mountain, selecting as we went the places right and left that seemed most advisable. At length we arrived, before nightfall, at the little town, where we put up at an inn for a few days.

15

Monastery and Legends

THERE is, in the land of the eastern Tibetans, a lamasery, the fame of which extends not merely throughout Tartary, but even to the remotest parts of Tibet. Thither pilgrims flock from all quarters, for there was born Tsong-Kaba, the famous reformer of Buddhism. The lamasery bears the name of Kumbum, and its lama population numbers no fewer than four thousand persons. It was determined that we should visit this place and endeavor to engage a lama to teach us, for a few months, the Tibetan language. Accordingly, there we took up our abode, and applied ourselves to study with perfect enthusiasm under the direction of our lama teacher, Sandara the Bearded, one of the inmates of the lamasery. During our stay we had ample leisure to study the country about us and the customs of its people. The country situated south of Koko-nor is inhabited by eastern Tibetans, who, like the Tartar-Mongols, lead a pastoral and nomadic life. In this beautiful, mountainous country Tsong-Kaba was born.

According to legend, at the age of three Tsong-Kaba resolved to renounce the world and to embrace the religious life. His mother, full of respect for the holy project of her son, shaved his head and threw his fine, long, flowing hair outside the tent. From this hair there forthwith sprang a tree, the wood of which dispensed an exquisite perfume, and each leaf of which bore, engraved on its surface, a character in the sacred language of Tibet. Tsong-Kaba himself withdrew into the most absolute retirement, avoiding even the presence of his parents. He took up his position on the summits of the wildest mountains, or in the depths of the profoundest ravines, and there passed whole days and nights in prayer and in the contemplation of eternal things. His fastings were long and frequent. He respected the life of even the humblest insect and rigorously denied himself the consumption of any sort of flesh whatsoever.

While Tsong-Kaba was thus engaged in purifying his heart by assiduous prayer and the practices of an austere life, a lama from one of the most remote regions of the west casually visited the land and received hospitality. Tsong-Kaba, amazed at the learning and the sanctity of the stranger, prostrated himself at his feet and conjured him to become his instructor. The lamaistic traditions relate that this lama of the western regions was remarkable not only for his learning, the profundity of which was unfathomable, but for the singularity of his appearance. People especially remarked his great nose and his eyes that gleamed as with a supernatural fire. The stranger, being on his part not less struck with the marvelous qualities of Tsong-Kaba, did not hesitate to adopt him as his disciple, and for this purpose took up his abode in the neighborhood. However, he lived there only a few years; after having initiated his pupil in all the doctrines recognized by the most renowned saints of the west, he fell asleep one day, on a stone, on the summit of a mountain, and his eyes opened not again.

Tsong-Kaba, deprived of the holy stranger's lessons, became all the more eager for religious instruction, and ere long he formed the resolution to abandon his tribe and go to the far west, to drink at their very source the pure precepts of sacred science. He departed alone, staff in hand and without a guide, but with his heart filled with superhuman courage. At last he arrived at the Land of Spirits (Lhasa) and selected a humble dwelling in the most solitary quarter of the town.

Despite his secluded residence, however, the monk soon attracted disciples; and before long his new doctrine, and the innovations which he introduced into the lamas' ceremonies, created considerable excitement. At length, Tsong-Kaba resolutely put himself forward as a reformer and began to make war upon the ancient worship. His partisans increased from day to day, and eventually they became known as the Yellow Cap Lamas. The reforms proposed by Tsong-Kaba were adopted throughout Tibet, and afterwards, by imperceptible degrees, were established in all the kingdoms of Tartary. In 1409, Tsong-Kaba, then fifty-two years old, founded the celebrated monastery of Galdan, three leagues from Lhasa. It still flourishes and contains upwards of eight thousand lamas. In 1419, the soul of Tsong-Kaba, who had supposedly become perfect, quitted the earth and returned to the Celestial Realm.

Upon the most superficial examination of the reforms and innovations introduced by Tsong-Kaba into Lamaism, one must be struck with their affinity to Catholicism. The cross, the miter, the dalmatic, the cope, which the Grand Lamas wear on their journeys or when they are performing some ceremony out of the temple; the service with double choirs, the psalmody, the exorcisms; the censer, suspended from five chains, which can be opened or closed at will; the benedictions given by the lamas extending the right hand over the heads of the faithful; ecclesiastical celibacy, spiritual retirement, the veneration of saints, the fasts, the processions, the chaplet, the litanies, the holy water—all these are analogies between the Buddhists and ourselves.

Now, can it be said that these analogies are of Christian origin? We think so. We have indeed not found, either in the traditions or in the monuments of the country, any positive proof of their adoption; still, it is perfectly legitimate to put forward conjectures which possess all the characteristics of the most emphatic probability. If one reflects that Tsong-Kaba lived at exactly the period when the Christian religion was being introduced into Central Asia, it will no longer be a matter of astonishment that we find, in reformed Buddhism, such striking analogies to Christianity.

And may we not proceed to lay down a proposition of a more positive character? This very legend of Tsong-Kaba, which we heard in the place of his birth and from the mouths of several lamas—does it not materially strengthen our theory? Setting aside all the marvelous features which have been added to the story by the imagination of the lamas, it may be fairly admitted that Tsong-Kaba was a man raised above the ordinary level by his genius, and also, perhaps by his virtue; that he was instructed by a stranger from the west; that after the death of the master, the disciple, proceeding to the west, took up his abode in Tibet, where he diffused the instruction which he himself had received. May it not be reasonably inferred that this stranger with the great nose was a European, one of those Catholic missioners who in that very period penetrated in such numbers into northern Asia?

It is by no means surprising that the lamas' traditions should have preserved the memory of that European face, whose type is so different from that of the Asiatics. We had more than once heard the lamas make remarks about the singularity of our features, and say that we must be of the same land as the master of Tsong-Kaba. It may be further supposed that a premature death did not permit the Catholic missioner to complete the religious education of his disciple; and that the latter, when afterwards he became an apostle, merely applied himself, whether from having acquired only an incomplete knowledge of Christian doctrine, or from having apostatized from it, to the introduction of a new Buddhist liturgy.

It will here be naturally expected that we say something about the miraculous tree which is supposed to have sprung from Tsong-Kaba's hair. This tree does exist, and we had heard of it too often during our journey not to feel

somewhat eager to visit it. We were told that it is at the foot of the mountain on which the lamasery stands, not far from the principal Buddhist temple, in a great square enclosure formed by brick walls.

Upon entering this enclosure, we were able to examine at leisure the marvelous tree, some of the branches of which had already grown above the wall. Our eyes were first directed with earnest curiosity to the leaves, and we were filled with absolute consternation on finding that, in point of fact, there were upon each of the leaves well-formed Tibetan characters, all of a green color, some darker, some lighter, than the leaf itself. Our first impression was a suspicion of fraud on the part of the lamas; but, after a minute examination of every detail, we could not discover the least deception. The characters all appeared to us portions of the leaf itself, equally with its veins. The position was not the same in all: in one leaf the character was at the top of the leaf; in another, in the middle; in a third, at the base, or at the side; the younger leaves represented the characters only in a partial state of formation.

The bark of the tree and its branches, which resemble that of the plane tree, are also covered with these characters. When a piece of old bark is removed, the young bark under it exhibits the indistinct outlines of characters in a germinating state, and, which is very singular, these new characters are not infrequently different from those which they replace. We examined everything with the closest attention, in order to detect some trace of trickery, but we could discern nothing of the sort. Perspiration actually trickled down our faces under the influence of the sensations which this most amazing spectacle created. More profound intellects than ours may, perhaps, be able to supply a satisfactory explanation of the mysteries of this singular tree; but as for us, we altogether give it up. Our readers possibly may smile at our ignorance; but we care not, so long as the sincerity and truth of our statement be not suspected.

This Tree of the Ten Thousand Images seemed to us of great age. Its trunk, which three men could scarcely encircle with outstretched arms, is not more than eight feet high; the branches, instead of shooting up, spread out in the shape of a plume of feathers, and are extremely bushy. A few branches are dead; the leaves are always green; and the wood, which is of a reddish tint, has an exquisite odor, something like that of cinnamon. The lamas informed us that in summer, towards the eighth moon, the tree produces large red flowers of an extremely beautiful character. They informed us also that there nowhere exists another such tree; that many attempts have been made in various lamaseries of Tartary and Tibet to propagate it by seeds and cuttings, but that all these attempts have been fruitless.

16
Stay Among the Lamas

D URING our stay at the lamasery, we occupied ourselves in the translation of an abridgment of sacred history from the creation of the world to the preachings of the Apostles. We gave to this work the dialogue form, the two interlocutors being a lama of the Lord of Heaven and a lama of Buddha. Sandara fulfilled his functions altogether as a matter of business. Religious feelings had no hold upon his grasping, hardened heart: he had a sneering, cold-blooded, carping incredulity, which he seemed to delight in parading upon all occasions. In his estimation, all religions were so many devices invented by the wise for the more facile and effective despoilment of the witless. Virtue, with him, was a vain word, and the man of merit was he who made more profit out of life than others.

Despite, however, these skeptical and impious opinions, Sandara could not prevent himself from feeling high admiration for the Christian doctrine. He was especially struck with the unity and sequence of the historical facts which he translated for us. He found in them a character of authenticity, of which the fables accumulated in the Buddhist books are wholly destitute; he admitted this, not infrequently, but always in an unguarded moment, for his aim was to maintain in our presence his melancholy role of freethinker. When he was with the lamas, however, he was more at his ease; and there he did not hesitate to declare

85

that, as to religious doctrine, we knew more about it than all the living Buddhas put together.

After some time we began to make a certain sensation in the lamasery: the lamas talked a good deal to one another about the two lamas of the western heaven and the new doctrine they taught. It was remarked that we were never seen to prostrate ourselves before Buddha; that, thrice a day, we said our prayers which were not Tibetan prayers; that we had a language of our own, which nobody else understood, but that with other people we talked Tartar, Chinese, and a little Tibetan. Here was more than enough to excite the curiosity of the lamas. Every day we had visitors, and the conversation with them always and altogether turned upon religious questions. Among all the lamas who visited us, we did not find one of the same incredulous stamp as Sandara the Bearded: on the contrary, they all seemed sincerely religious and full of faith; many of them attached the utmost importance to the study and knowledge of truth; and we found the same men coming again and again to seek instruction in our holy religion.

The instruction we communicated was altogether historical in its plan, everything being carefully excluded which could suggest dispute or arouse the spirit of contention. We gave our friends a simple and concise outline of our religion, leaving them to derive thence, for themselves, conclusions against Buddhism. Proper names and dates, exactly set forth, produced more effect upon them than the most logical reasoning. When they had throughly mastered the names of Jesus, of Jerusalem, of Pontius Pilate, the date of the creation of the world—four thousand years before Christ, and the names of the Twelve Apostles, they had no longer any doubts as to the redemption, or as to the preaching of the Gospel. The connection which they observed between the history of the Old Testament and that of the New amounted, in their eyes, to proof. The mysteries and the miracles created no difficulty in their minds.

The eagerness of the lamas to visit us, and especially their favorable attitude towards Christianity, gave, after a while, umbrage to Sandara: he turned desperately sulky, and after going through the lesson of the day, in the dryest and briefest manner possible, he would say not another word to us for the rest of the twenty-four hours, but observed towards us the most contumelious silence. If we asked him, in the humblest manner, the Tibetan name of some object or the meaning of some particular phrase in the dialogues, he would not even deign to answer our question.

In this extremity we usually had recourse to a neighbor, a young student of medicine, who always gave us the information we needed with the most frank cordiality; and, although he was not very learned in Tibetan, we found him of very great use. His open, good-natured character, moreover, encouraged us to ask him many questions respecting some of the lama practices which we desired to understand. In return for these services, we aided, with all our hearts, his desire to become acquainted with the Christian religion. Far different from Sandara, he was full of respect for the truths we announced to him; but his timid, irresolute temperament kept him from openly abjuring Buddhism. His idea was that he could be, at one and the same time, a good Christian and a fervent Buddhist: in his prayers he invoked alternately Tsong-Kaba and the Lord of Heaven, and he carried his simplicity so far as to ask us sometimes to take part in his religious practices.

One day he proposed to us a practice of devotion in favor of all the travelers throughout the whole world. "We are not acquainted with this devotion," said we. "Will you explain it to us?"

"This is it. You know that a good many travelers find themselves, from time to time, on rugged, toilsome roads. Some of these travelers are holy lamas on a pilgrimage, and it often happens that they cannot proceed by reason of their being altogether exhausted. In this case we aid them by sending horses to them."

"That," said we, "is a most admirable custom, entirely conformable with the principles of Christian charity. But you must consider that poor travelers, such as we, are not in a position to participate in the good work; you know that we possess only a horse and a little mule, which require rest, in order that they may carry us into Tibet."

"Tsong-Kaba!" ejaculated the lama, and then he clapped his hands together and burst into a loud laugh.

"What are you laughing at? What we have said is the simple truth: we have only a horse and a little mule."

When his laughter at last subsided, "I was not laughing at that," said he. "I laughed at your misconceiving the sort of devotion I mean. We send the travelers paper horses!"

And therewith he ran off to his cell, leaving us with an excellent occasion for laughing in our turn at the charity of the Buddhists, which we thus learned consisted in giving paper horses to travelers. We maintained our gravity, however, for we had made it a rule never to ridicule the practices of the lamas. Presently our friend returned, his hands filled with bits of paper, on each of which was printed the figure of a horse, saddled and bridled, and going at full gallop.

"Here!" cried he. "These are the horses we send to the travelers. Tomorrow we shall ascend a high mountain, thirty li from the lamasery, and there we shall pass the day, saying prayers and sending off horses."

"How do you send them to the travelers?"

"Oh, the means are very easy! After a certain form of prayer, we take a packet of horses and throw them up into the air; the wind carries them away; and by the power of Buddha they are then changed into real horses, which offer themselves to travelers."

We candidly told our dear neighbor what we thought of this practice, and explained to him the grounds upon which we declined to take any part in it. He seemed to approve of our sentiments on the subject; but this approval did not prevent him from spending a large portion of the night in making, by means of the printing-press, a prodigious number of horses. Next morning, before daybreak, he went off, accompanied by several colleagues, who were full, like himself, of devotion for poor travelers. They carried with them a tent, a boiler, and some provisions.

All the morning the wind blew a hurricane. When, towards noon, this subsided, the sky became dark and heavy, and the snow fell in thick flakes. We awaited, with anxious impatience, the return of our friend. The poor wretch returned in the evening, quite worn out with cold and fatigue. We invited him to rest for awhile in our tent, and we gave him some tea with milk, and some rolls fried in butter. "It has been a dreadful day!" said he.

"Yes, the wind blew here with great violence."

"I'll venture to affirm it was nothing here to what we found it on the top of the mountain! The tent, the boiler—and everything we had with us—were carried away by a regular whirlwind, and we were obliged to throw ourselves flat on the ground in order to save ourselves from being carried away, too."

"It's a sad pity you've lost your tent and boiler."

"It is, indeed, a misfortune. However, it must be admitted that the weather was very favorable for conveying horses to the travelers. When we saw that it was going to snow, we threw the horses all up into the air at once, and the wind whisked them off to the four quarters of the world. If we had waited any longer, the snow would have wetted them, and they would have stuck on the sides of the mountain." Altogether, this excellent young man was not dissatisfied with his day's work.

The twenty-fifth of each moon is the day devoted to the transmission of horses to poor travelers. The practice is not a general rule but is left to the devotion of individuals. The

twenty-eighth of the moon is set apart for another species
of religious exercise, in which all the lamas are required to
participate. On the twenty-seventh our lama friend gave us
notice of the ceremony, in these words: "Tomorrow night
we shall, perhaps, prevent your sleeping, for we shall have
to celebrate our nocturnal prayers."

We paid no special attention to this intimation, conceiv-
ing it to mean that in the course of the night the lamas
would recite prayers in their cells, as they not infrequently
did. We accordingly retired to rest at our usual hour, and
fell asleep. In conformity with the warning, our slumbers
did not remain long uninterrupted. First we seemed to
dream that we heard a sort of concert by a great multitude of
voices up in the air. Gradually these vague, confused sounds
became loud and distinct. We awoke and heard clearly
enough the chanting of lamas' prayers. In the twinkling of
an eye, we were up and dressed and out in the courtyard,
which was illuminated with a pale light that appeared to
come from above.

In his wonted corner sat old Akayé, the master of the
house, telling his beads. "Akayé," we asked, "what is this
strange noise?"

"The nocturnal prayers. If you want to see more of them,
you had better go on the terrace."

There was a ladder resting in the most accommodating
manner against the wall. We hastily ascended it, and became spectators of a most singular sight. The terraces were
illuminated by red lanterns suspended from long poles, and
all the lamas, attired in their ceremonial mantles and yellow miters, were seated on the roofs of their houses, chanting their prayers in a slow monotonous voice. On the roof
of our own house we found our medical-student friend and
two other lamas, wholly absorbed in the ceremony. We took
care not to disturb them, and contented ourselves with
merely looking on and listening. Those innumerable lanterns, with their red, fantastic glare, the buildings of the

lamasery vaguely illumined by the reflection of their trembling light, the four thousand voices combining in one immense concert, accompanied from time to time by the sound of trumpets and conch horns—all this produced an effect that agitated the soul with a sort of vague terror.

After having gazed for awhile at this strange spectacle, we descended into the courtyard, where we found old Akayé still in the same place and the same position. "Well," said he, "you have seen the ceremony of nocturnal prayers?"

"Yes, but we don't understand the purpose of the prayers. Would it be troubling you too much to ask from you some explanation of the matter?"

"Not at all. These prayers were instituted for the purpose of driving away demons. You must know that this country was once fearfully infested with demons, who caused maladies in the herds and spoiled the milk of the cows. They often invaded the cells of the lamas, and at times carried their audacity to the excess of penetrating into the temple in the hour of general prayer, their presence being indicated by the confusion and discord which immediately prevailed in the psalmody. During the night they assembled in large numbers in the ravine, where they frightened everybody with cries and howlings so strange in their character that no man could imitate them. A lama, full of learning and piety, invented the nocturnal prayers—and the demons have since almost entirely disappeared from the district. A few come here occasionally, but they don't do any such mischief as they used to do."

"Akayé," asked we, "have you ever chanced to see any of these demons?"

"No, never; and I am sure you have not seen any of them."

"What makes you suppose so?"

"Because the demons appear only to wicked lamas; the good lamas never see them."

At this moment the prayer of the lamas on the housetops

ceased; the trumpets, the bells, the drums, and the conches sounded all at once three different times; the lamas then all sent forth together hideous cries and yells, like those of wild beasts; and the ceremony terminated. The lanterns were extinguished, and silence resumed its sway. We bade old Akayé good night, and once more went to sleep.

17

Move to Chu-khor-tang

WE resided at Kumbum more than three months, enjoying the friendly sympathies of the Buddhist monks and the protection of the authorities. But for some time we had been actually violating an important rule of the lamasery. Strangers who pass through Kumbum, or who merely reside there for a short time, may dress as they please. Those persons, on the contrary, who are connected in any way with the lamasery, or who are staying long in the place, are required to wear the sacred dress of the lamas; that is to say, a red gown, a small dalmatic, without sleeves and showing the arm, a red scarf, and a yellow miter. This rule of uniformity is very strictly enforced; and accordingly, one fine morning, the master of discipline sent an official formally to request that we observe the statutes of the lamasery. We replied that, not being of the religion of Buddha, we could not adopt the sacred dress—that is, the liturgical garb—of the lamas without insulting our own holy religion; but that, as we did not wish to create the slightest confusion in the establishment, we were ready to quit it, if we could not obtain a dispensation in the matter of costume.

Several days passed without anything further being said on this unpleasant subject. Meantime Samdadchiemba arrived with the three camels, which he had been pasturing in a valley of Koko nor. If we should have to depart, it was clear that his return was most opportune. By-and-by, the governing body of the lamas once more sent us their envoy, to say that the rule of the lamasery was inflexible; that they grieved that our sublime and sacred religion did not permit us to comply with it; but that, although we could not remain in the lamasery of Kumbum, they would gladly retain us in the neighborhood, and that to this end they invited us to go and take up our abode at Chu-khor-tang, where we might wear what dress we pleased.

We had heard a great deal about the little lamasery of Chu-khor-tang, which serves as a sort of country house and botanical garden for the faculty of medicine. It stands within half an hour's walk of Kumbum. The Grand Lamas and students of the medical section go there every year, towards the close of summer, and remain generally for about a fortnight, collecting medicinal plants on the surrounding hills. During the remainder of the year most of the houses are empty, and one scarcely sees a single soul, except for a few contemplative lamas who have hollowed out cells for themselves in the most rugged declivities of the mountain.

The proposition of the ruling lamas appeared to us altogether desirable, for the fine weather was just setting in: winter in town, spring in the country—this was admirable! Our three months' abode in Kumbum had made us tolerably conversant with lama manners: we accordingly purchased a *khata*, or "scarf of happiness," and a small dish of raisins, with which we repaired to the lama administrator of Chu-khor-tang. The *khata* is a piece of white silk, indispensable to rich and poor: if one goes to pay a visit of ceremony, or to ask a service, or to return thanks for a favor, he must always begin by presenting a *khata* to the person to be honored. The administrator received us in the most affable manner and promised at once to give orders for the preparation of a suitable abode for us. After giving a splendid feast of farewell to old Akayé, and the few other special friends we had made among the lamas of Kumbum, we loaded our camels with our baggage and gaily proceeded on our way to the little lamasery.

A half hour sufficed for us to effect our removal to Chu-khor-tang. After skirting for some time the arid sides of a lofty mountain, we descended into a broad valley, through which flowed a rivulet, the banks of which were still covered with ice. The place seemed full of good pasturage, but, because of the coldness of the climate, vegetation is always very slow and very late in the locality. Although it was near the month of May, the young seedlings raising their heads above the ground scarcely gave the valley a yellowish tinge.

A lama with red, round face, came to meet us, and conducted us to the habitation which the administrator of the lamascry had prepared for our reception. We were installed in a large apartment which, only the evening before, had served as the abode of sundry juvenile calves, too young and too weak to follow the parent cows to the mountains. Pains had been taken to clean the apartment, but the success had not been so perfect as to preclude our distinguishing on the floor many traces of the late occupants. However, the authorities had assigned to us the best accommodation that the lamasery afforded.

We had frequent conversations with the contemplative lamas, but we could never exactly ascertain what it was they contemplated up there in their nests. They themselves could give nothing like a clear idea of the matter; they had embraced this manner of life, they told us, because they had read in their books that lamas of very great sanctity had lived in that way. However, they were worthy folk, of peaceful, simple, easy temperaments, who passed their waking hours in prayer, and, when tired of praying they found in sleep an honest relaxation.

Besides these five hermits, who always dwelt in the rocks above, there were below several lamas who had charge of the unoccupied houses of the lamasery. These by no means looked at life in its refined and mystical aspect; they were, in fact, herdsmen. In the great house where we lived, there were two big lamas who poetically passed their time in herding some twenty cattle, in milking the cows, making butter and cheese, and looking after the calves. These bucolics seemed little given to contemplation or prayer: they sent forth, indeed, frequent invocations to Tsong-Kaba, but this was always on account of their beasts, because their cows multiplied and would not be milked, or because the calves capered out of bounds over the valley.

Our arrival afforded these herdsmen a little diversion from the monotony of pastoral life. They often paid us a visit in our chamber, and always passed in review the volumes of our small traveling library, with that timid and respectful curiosity which simple and illiterate persons ever manifest towards the productions of the intellect. When they found us writing, they forgot cows and calves and milk and cheese and butter, and sometimes stood motionless for hours together, their eyes fixed upon our crow-quill pen as it ran over the paper and left impressed there characters, the delicacy and novelty of which were matters of ecstatic amazement to these simple creatures.

The little lamasery of Chu-khor-tang pleased us beyond our hopes. We never once regretted Kumbum, any more than the prisoner regrets his dungeon after he has attained liberty. The reason was that we, too, felt ourselves emancipated. We were no longer under the rod of Sandara the Bearded, that hard and pitiless taskmaster who, while giving us lessons in Tibetan, seemed to have undertaken also to discipline us in patience and humility. The desire to attain knowledge had made us submit to his ill treatment, but our departure from Kumbum afforded a joyful opportunity of throwing off this leech who, for five whole months had remained obstinately attached to our existence. Besides, the modest success we had already achieved in the study of the

Tibetan tongue exempted us from the future necessity of having a master at our shoulders; we were quite strong enough to walk alone and unaided.

Our hours of labor were employed in revising and analyzing our dialogues, and in translating a small Tibetan work entitled "Forty-two Points of Instruction, Delivered by Buddha." We possessed a magnificent edition of this work, in four languages—Tibetan, Mongol, Manchu, and Chinese; so that, thus aided, we had no occasion to refer to the learning of the lamas. When the Tibetan version presented any difficulty, all we had to do, in order to remove such, was to consult the three other versions, with which we were passably acquainted.

Our first days at Chu-khor-tang were entirely devoted to the translation of the "Book of Buddha," but we soon found ourselves compelled to devote a portion of our time to the occupations of pastoral life. We had noticed that every evening our animals returned half starved, that, instead of growing fatter and fatter, they were daily becoming leaner and leaner. The simple reason was that Samdadchiemba took no sort of pains to find pasturage for them. After driving them out somewhere or other, he cared not where, he would leave them to themselves on some arid hillside, and he would go to sleep in the sun or stroll about chatting and tea-drinking in the black tents. It was to no purpose we lectured him; he went on just the same as before—his reckless, independent character having undergone no modification whatever. Our only mode of remedying the evil was to turn herdsmen ourselves.

Moreover, it was impossible to remain obstinately and exclusively men of letters when all around seemed inviting us to make some concessions to the habits of this pastoral people. The herds of the eastern Tibetans consist of sheep, goats, and long-haired cattle; these people do not breed as many horses as the Tartars, but those which they do breed are stronger and better formed. The camels which we find in their country belong, for the most part, to the Tartar-Mongols.

The variety of long-haired cattle called in Chinese *Tchang-Mao-Nieou*, is called *yak* by the Tibetans, *sarligue* by the Tartars, and *boeuf grognant* by the French naturalists. The cry of this animal does, in fact, resemble the grunting of a hog; but it is louder in tone and longer in duration. The yak is short and thick, and not so big as an ordinary ox; its hair is long, fine, and shiny—that under the body actually trails on the ground. Its hoofs are small and crooked, like those of goats; and, like the goat, it delights in clambering up rocks and standing upon the edge of the most rugged precipices. When at play, it twists and turns its tail, which terminates in a broad tuft like a plume of feathers. The flesh is excellent; the milk delicious; and butter made of that milk is beyond all praise.

18
Tibetan Friends and Customs

ONE day a lama herdsman, who lived in the same house with us, came, with a long, dismal face, to announce that one of his cows had calved during the night. The calf had died in the course of the day. The lama forthwith skinned the poor beast and stuffed it with hay. This proceeding surprised us at first, for the lama had by no means the air of a man likely to give himself the luxury of a cabinet of natural history. When the operation was completed, we observed that the hay calf had neither feet nor head; thereupon it occurred to us that, after all, it was merely a pillow that the lama contemplated. We were in error; but the error was not dispelled until the next morning, when our herdsman went to milk the cow.

When we saw him come forth, his pail in one hand, the hay calf under the other arm, the fancy occurred to us to follow him. His first proceeding was to put the hay calf down before the cow; then he began the milking. The cow at first opened enormous eyes at her beloved infant; by degrees, she stooped her head towards it, then smelt it, sneezed three or four times, and at last proceeded to lick it with the most delightful tenderness. This spectacle grated against our sensibilities: it seemed to us that he who first invented this parody upon one of the most touching incidents in nature must have been a man without a heart. A somewhat burlesque circumstance occurred one day to modify the indignation with which this trickery inspired us. By dint of caressing and licking her little calf, the tender parent one fine morning ripped it; the hay issued from within, and the cow, manifesting not the smallest surprise or agitation, proceeded tranquilly to devour the unexpected provender.

One day, while our camels were tranquilly browsing on some thorny shrubs in the depths of the valley, we sought an asylum from the north wind in a small tent, whence issued a thick smoke. We found in it an old man who, with knees and hands on the ground, was puffing with all his might at a heap of *argols* which he had just placed on the fire. We seated ourselves on a yak skin. The old man crossed his legs, and held out his hand to us. We gave him our teacups, which he filled with milk tea, saying, "*Temouchi* (drink in peace)."

He then gazed at us alternately, with an air of some anxiety. "*Aka* (Brother)," said we, "this is the first time we have come to seat ourselves in your tent."

"I am old," he replied; "my legs will scarce sustain me. Otherwise, I should have gone to Chu-khor-tang to offer you my *khata*. According to what the shepherds of the black tents have told me, you are from the farther western heaven."

"Yes, our country is far hence."

"Are you from the kingdom of the Samba, or from that of the Poba?"

"From neither; we come from the kingdom of the French."

"Ah, you are French? I never before heard of them. 'Tis such a great place, that west! The kingdoms there are so numerous. But, after all, it matters not: we are all of the same family, are we not?"

"Yes, assuredly all men are brothers, in whatever kingdom each is born."

"That is true. What you say is founded on reason; all men

are brothers. Yet we know that, under heaven, there exist three great families: the Chinese, the Tibetan, and the Tartar. We men of this west are all of the great Tibetan family; that's what I wanted to say."

"*Aka*, do you know whence come the three great families that are beneath heaven?"

"This is what I have heard from lamas learned in the things of antiquity. In the beginning, there was on the earth but one single man. He had neither house nor tent; for in those days winter was not cold, nor summer hot; the wind did not blow with violence, and there fell neither rain nor snow; tea grew of itself on the mountains; and the cattle had nothing to fear from malevolent animals. This man had three children, who lived a long time with him, feeding upon milk and fruits. After attaining a very great age, this man died. The three children consulted on what they should do with the body of their father. They could not agree on the point, for each had a different opinion. One of them wanted to put him in a coffin, and bury him; the second proposed to burn him; the third said it would be better to expose him on the top of a mountain.

"In the end, they resolved to cut the body into three pieces, to take each of them one piece, and then to separate. The eldest received the head and arms for his share. He was the ancestor of the great Chinese family; and this is why his descendants have become celebrated in arts and industry, and remarkable for their intelligence and for the devices and stratagems they can invent. The youngest, who was the father of the great Tibetan family, had the chest and stomach for his share; and this is why the Tibetans are full of heart and courage, fearing not to encounter death, and ever having among them indomitable tribes. The middle son, from whom descended the Tartar peoples, received as his inheritance the lower part of the body. You, who have traveled much in the deserts of the east, must know that the Mongols are simple and timid, without head and without heart; their only merit consists in keeping themselves firm on their stirrups and solid on their saddles.

"This is how the lamas explain the origin of the three great families that are beneath heaven, and the difference in their characters. This is why the Tartars are good horsemen; the Tibetans, good soldiers; and the Chinese, good traders."

As a return to the old man for his interesting chronicle, we related to him the history of the first man, Adam, of the Deluge, and of Noah and his three children. He was at first extremely pleased to find in our story also his three great families; but his surprise was immense when he heard us state that the Chinese, the Tartars, and the Tibetans are all children of Shem; and that, besides these, there are innumerable nations who compose the two other families, those of Cham and Japhet. Our auditor looked at us fixedly, his mouth half open, and his head from time to time thrown up in amazement, as much as to say, "I never thought the world was so big!"

The time had passed rapidly during this archaeological sitting; so, after saluting the old man, we went to our camels and rode home to Chu-khor-tang. There, fastening our mounts to a stake at the door of our residence, we proceeded into our humble kitchen to prepare our evening meal.

Culinarily speaking, we were far better off at Chu-khor-tang than at Kumbum. In the first place, we had milk, curds, butter, and cheese. Then we had discovered a perfect treasure in a hunter of the vicinity. A few days after our arrival, this Nimrod entered our room, and, taking a magnificent hare from a bag he carried at his back, asked us whether the lamas of the western heaven ate the flesh of wild animals.

"Certainly," said we; "and we consider hares very nice. Don't you eat them?"

"We laymen do, sometimes, but the lamas, never. They

are expressly forbidden by the Book of Prayers to eat black flesh."

"The sacred law of the Lord of the western heaven has prescribed no such prohibition to us."

"In that case keep the animal; and, as you like hares, I will bring you as many of them every day as you please. The hills about Chu-khor-tang are completely covered with them."

Just at this point a lama chanced to enter our apartment. When he saw, stretched at our feet, the still warm and bleeding form of the hare, "Tsong-Kaba! Tsong-Kaba!" exclaimed he, starting back with a gesture of horror and veiling his eyes with both hands. Then, after launching a malediction against the poor hunter, he asked us whether we should dare to eat that black flesh.

"Why not," rejoined we, "since it can injure neither our bodies nor our souls?" And thereupon, we laid down certain principles of morality, explaining that the eating of venison is, in itself, no obstacle to the acquisition of sanctity.

The hunter was highly delighted with our dissertation; the lama was altogether confounded. The latter contented himself with saying, by way of reply, that in us, who were foreigners and of the religion of the west, it might be no harm to eat hares; but that the lamas must abstain from it because, if they failed to observe the prohibition and their dereliction became known to the Grand Lama, they would be pitilessly expelled from the lamasery.

Our thesis having been thus victoriously sustained, we next proceeded to consider the proposition of the hunter, to provide us every day with as many hares as we pleased. First, we asked him whether he was in earnest. Upon his replying in the affirmative, we told him that every morning he might bring us a hare, but on the understanding that we were to pay him for it.

"We don't sell hares here," replied he; "but since you will not accept them gratuitously, you shall give me for each the

value of a gun charge." We insisted upon a more liberal
scale of remuneration, and at last it was arranged that, for
every piece of game he brought us, we should give him forty
sapeks, the equivalent of about four French sous.

We decided upon eating hares for two reasons: first,
as a matter of conscience, in order to prevent the lamas
from imagining that we permitted ourselves to be influenced
by the prejudices of the sectaries of Buddha; and secondly,
as a matter of economy, for a hare cost infinitely less than
our insipid barley meal.

One day our indefatigable hunter brought us, instead of
a hare, an immense roebuck, which is also black flesh and
prohibited. In order not to conform in the least degree with
Buddhist superstitions, we purchased the roebuck, for the
sum of three hundred sapeks (thirty French sous). Our
chimney smoked with venison preparations for eight con-
secutive days, and all that time Samdadchiemba was in a
most amiable frame of mind.

Lest we should contract habits too exclusively carnivo-
rous, we resolved to introduce the vegetable kingdom into
our daily meals. In the desert this was no easy matter. However, by dint of industry combined with experience, we
ultimately discovered some wild plants, which, dressed in
a particular manner, were by no means to be despised. We
were able to enjoy a delightful variety of wild herbs from
the hills for more than a month. Then the little tubercles
of the fern became hollow and horny, and the stems themselves grew as hard as wood, while the nettles, armed with
a long white beard, presented only a menacing and awful
aspect. Later in the year, when the season was more advanced, the perfumed strawberry of the mountain and the
white mushroom of the valley became invaluable substi-
tutes for fern and nettle. But we had to wait a long time
for these luxuries, the cold in these countries being of
protracted duration, and the vegetation, in consequence,
exceedingly late.

19

Mountain Summer

THROUGHOUT June snow still falls, and the wind is so cold that one cannot, without imprudence, throw aside one's fur coat. With the first days of July, the warmth of the sun begins to be felt, and the rain falls in heavy showers. No sooner does the sky clear up, than a warm vapor rises from the earth, in surprising abundance. One sees it first skimming the surface of the valleys and the low hills; then it condenses, and oscillates somewhat above the surface, becoming by degrees so thick that it obscures the light of day. When this vapor has ascended high enough in the air to form great clouds, the south wind rises, and the rain again pours down upon the earth. Then the sky becomes clear once more, and once more the vapor rises and rises; and so it goes on. These atmospheric revolutions continue for a fortnight. Meanwhile, the earth is in a sort of fermentation; all the animals keep crouching on the ground; and men, women, and children feel, in every limb, vague, indescribable discomfort and disability. This period is called the season of land vapors. Immediately that the crisis is past, the grass in the valley grows visibly, and the mountains and hills around are covered, as by enchantment, with flowers and verdure.

The period was also one of regeneration for our camels. They became wholly divested of their hair, which fell from them in large flakes, like rags, and for a few days they were as bare as though they had been closely shaved from the muzzle of the nose to the tip of the tail. In this condition they were perfectly hideous. In the shade they shook with cold in every limb, and at night we were obliged to cover them with great pieces of felt to keep them from dying of cold. After twenty days had elapsed, the hair began to re-appear. First it was merely a red down, extremely fine and curling, like lamb's wool. The intense ugliness of the animals during their state of nudity made them appear perfectly beautiful in their new attire, which was completed in a fortnight. Thus newly dressed, they rushed with ardor to the pastures, in order to build up respectable dimensions and adequate strength for their autumnal journey. To sharpen their appetites, we had purchased some sea salt, of which we gave them a large dose every morning before they went into the valley.

The new coating of our camels had enriched us with an immense quantity of hair. We exchanged one half of it for barley meal, and the question then arose as to what was the best use we could make of the remainder. A lama who was a skillful rope maker suggested an excellent idea: he pointed out that, during the long journey through Tibet, we should need a large supply of cord wherewith to fasten the luggage, and that ropes made of camel's hair were, on account of their flexibility, the best for cold countries. The suggestion, so full of wisdom, was at once adopted. The lama gave us, gratuitously, a few lessons in his art, and we set to work. In a very short time, we were able to twist our material tolerably well, so as to give it a form approximately, at least, resembling rope. Every day when we went out to tend our cattle, each of us took under his arm a bundle of camel's hair, which on his way he twisted into the smaller strings that, on our return, we combined into larger cords.

Samdadchiemba contented himself with looking on as we worked, and with an occasional smile at our slips. Partly through idleness, partly through vanity, he abstained from lending us a hand. "My spiritual fathers," said he, one day, "how can people of your quality demean yourselves by rope-making? Would it not be much more proper to buy what ropes you require, or to give the materials out to be made by persons in the trade?"

This question afforded us an opportunity of giving our cameleer a sound rating. After having emphatically impressed upon him that we were in no position to play the fine gentlemen, and that we must closely study economy, we cited to him the example of Saint Paul, who had thought it no derogation from his dignity to labor with his hands, in order to avoid being a burden to the faithful. As soon as Samdadchiemba learned that Saint Paul had been at the same time a currier and an apostle, he forthwith abandoned his idleness and self-sufficiency, and applied himself with ardor to rope-making. What was our astonishment, on seeing the fellow at work, to find that he was a first-rate braider, for not an inkling had he ever given us to that effect! He selected the finest wool, and with it wove bridles and halters that were really masterpieces. It is almost unnecessary to add that he was forthwith placed at the head of our rope-making establishment, and that we submitted ourselves altogether to his direction.

The fine weather brought to Chu-khor-tang a great number of visitors from Kumbum, who sought both a change of air and temporary relaxation from their studies. Our apartment now became a point of pilgrimage, for no one thought of spending a day at Chu-khor-tang without paying a visit to the lamas of the western heaven. Those lamas with whom we had formed a more intimate acquaintance at Kumbum, and who had begun to inform themselves as to the truths of the Christian religion, were attracted by a far higher motive than curiosity: they desired to discourse further of the holy doctrine of Christ and to seek from us explanations of difficulties which had occurred to them. Oh, how our hearts were penetrated with ineffable joy when we heard these Buddhist monks pronounce with respect the sacred names of Jesus and Mary, and recite, with manifest devotion, the prayers we had taught them. The great God, we doubt not, will place to their favorable account these first steps in the path of salvation, and will not fail to send shepherds to bring home to the fold these poor wandering sheep.

Among the lamas who came to recreate for a while at Chu-khor-tang, we remarked especially a number of Tartar-Mongols. These brought with them small tents, which they set up in the valley along the stream, or upon the sides of the most picturesque hills. There they passed whole days reveling in the delight of the independent life of the nomads, forgetting awhile the constraint and confinement of the lamaistic life in the enjoyment of the free life of the tent. One saw them running and frolicking about the prairie like children, or wrestling and exercising in other sports which recalled the days and the land of their boyhood. The reaction with many of these men became so strong that even fixity of tent became insupportable, and they would take their tents down and set them up again in some other place, three or four times a day; or they would even abandon tents altogether, and, taking their kitchen utensils and their pails of water and their provisions on their shoulders, would go, singing and dancing, to boil their tea on the summit of some mountain, from which they would not descend till nightfall.

20

On the Trail Again

TOWARDS September we received the joyful news that the Tibetan embassy had arrived at Tangar, and would remain there for several days, in order to lay in stock for provisions and arrange its order of march. Thus at last, after the long and annoying delay, we were about to proceed to the capital of Tibet. Without loss of time, we made all our necessary preparations. First we had to pay a visit to Kumbum, in order to purchase provisions for four months, since on the whole route there was not the least possibility of finding anything to buy that we should need. Upon a careful calculation, we decided that we should require five bricks of tea, two sheep's paunches of butter, two sacks of flour, and eight sacks of *tsamba*.

Tsamba is the name given here to barley meal, the insipid article which constitutes the ordinary food of the Tibetans. These people take a teacup half filled with boiling tea; to this they add some pinches of *tsamba* and then they mix these materials together with the finger, into a sort of wretched paste, neither cooked nor uncooked, hot or cold. This paste is then swallowed, and is considered breakfast, dinner, or supper, as the case may be. If a traveler desires to cross the desert to Lhasa, he must perforce resign himself to *tsamba*. 'Tis to no avail the French traveler sighs for his accustomed knife and fork, and his accustomed dishes: he must do without them.

Persons full of experience and philanthropy counseled

us to lay in a good store of garlic, and every day to chew
several cloves of it, unless we wished to be killed on our
way by the deleterious vapors that emanated from certain
elevated mountains. We did not discuss the merits of this
hygienic advice, but adopted it with absolute confidence.

Our residence in the valley of Chu-khor-tang had been
in a high degree advantageous to our animals, which had
become fatter than we had ever before known them. The
camels, in particular, were magnificently stout; their humps,
made firm with solid flesh, rose proudly on their backs, and
seemed to defy the fatigues and privations of the desert.
Still, even in their improved condition, three camels were
not enough to carry our provisions and our baggage. We
accordingly added to our caravan a supplementary camel
and horse, which lightened our exchequer to the extent
of twenty-five ounces of silver; moreover, we hired a young
lama of the Ratchie mountains, with whom we had become
acquainted at Kumbum, and who was admitted into our
party in the capacity of assistant cameleer. This appoint-
ment, while it raised the social standing of Samdadchiemba,
diminished also the fatigues of his functions.

According to this new arrangement, the little caravan was
disposed in the following order: the assistant cameleer,
Charadchambeul, went on foot, and led after him the four
camels, which marched in Indian file, the one fastened to
the tail of the other; Samdadchiemba, cameleer-in-chief,
rode his little black mule beside the camels; and the two
missioners closed the procession, each mounted on a white
horse. After having exchanged infinite *khatas* with our acquaintances and friends at Kumbum and Chu-khor-tang,
we proceeded on our route, directing our march towards
the Blue Sea, where we were to await the Tibetan embassy.

From Chu-khor-tang to the Koko nor was four days'
march. We passed on our way a small lamasery, called Tansan, containing at most two hundred lamas. Its site is perfectly enchanting; rocky mountains, covered with shrubs

and tall firs, form for it a circular enclosure, in the center of which rise the habitations of the lamas. A stream, bordered with willows and fine longwort, after tranquilly encircling the lamasery, dashes over a rocky fall and continues its course in the desert. The Buddhist monastery of Tansan is, they say, very rich, being largely endowed by the Mongol princes of Koko nor.

On leaving the lamasery of Tansan, we entered an extensive plain, where numerous Mongol tents and flocks of every kind picturesquely variegated the verdure of the pastures. We met two lamas on horseback, who were seeking contributions of butter from the wealthy shepherds of the locality. Their procedure is this: they present themselves at the entrance of each tent, and thrice sound a conch horn. Thereupon, some member of the family brings out a small roll of butter, which, without saying a word, he deposits in a bag, suspended from the saddle of each lama's horse. The lamas never once alight, but content themselves with riding up to each tent, and announcing their presence to the inmates by the sound of the shell.

As we advanced, the country became more fertile and less mountainous, until at length we reached the vast and magnificent pasturage of Koko nor. There vegetation is so vigorous, that the grass rose up to the stomachs of our camels. Soon we discovered far before us, quite on the horizon, what seemed a broad silver ribbon, above which floated light vapors that, rising, became lost in the azure of the heavens. Our assistant cameleer informed us that this was the Blue Sea. His words filled us with a tremulous joy; we urged on our animals, and the sun had not set when we planted our tent within a hundred paces of the waters of the great lake.

The Blue Lake—in Mongol Koko nor—was originally called by the Chinese the Western Sea; now they call it the Blue Sea. This immense reservoir of water, which is more than a hundred leagues in circumference, seems, in fact, to merit the title of sea, rather than merely that of lake. Not only is it of vast extent, but its waters are bitter and salt, like those of the ocean, and undergo, in a similar manner, ebb and flow. The marine odor which they exhale is smelled at a great distance, far into the desert.

Towards the western portion of the Blue Sea there is a small island, rocky and bare, inhabited by twenty contemplative lamas, who have built thereon a Buddhist temple and some modest habitations. There they pass their lives in tranquil retirement, far from the distracting disquietudes of the world. No one can go and visit them, for, throughout the entire extent of the lake, there is not a single boat of any kind to be seen; at all events we saw none, and the Mongols told us that among their tribes no one ever thought of occupying himself in any way with navigation. In the winter, indeed, at the time of the more intense cold, the water is frozen solidly enough to enable the shepherds around to repair in pilgrimage to the lamasery. They bear to the contemplative lamas their modest offerings of butter, tea, and tsamba, and receive, in exchange, benedictions and prayers for good pasturage and prosperous flocks.

We abode in Koko nor for nearly a month. Continual rumors of brigands compelled us to move our encampment five or six times, in order to follow the Tartar tribes. These at the least suggestion of approaching assailants, change their quarters, taking care, however, never to depart altogether from the rich pastures which border the Blue Sea. Towards the end of October, the Tibetan embassy arrived, and we joined the immense body. It was already augmented by a great number of Mongol caravans which, like ourselves, availed themselves of this favorable escort to Lhasa.

21

With the Caravan

NEXT day, after our departure from Koko nor we placed ourselves at the front of the caravan, and then halted on one side, in order to see the immense procession pass before us and so make acquaintance with our traveling companions. The men and animals composing the caravan might be thus estimated: fifteen thousand long-haired oxen, twelve hundred horses, twelve hundred camels, and two thousand men—Tibetans and Tartars, some on foot, some on ox-back, but most of them on horses and camels. All the cavalry were armed with lances, sabers, bows and arrows, and matchlocks.

The general march and particular movements of the caravan were executed with tolerable order and precision, especially at the outset. Generally we started every morning two or three hours before sunrise, in order that we might encamp about noon and give the animals full time to feed during the remainder of the day. The reveille was announced by a cannon shot; forthwith, everybody rose, the fires were lighted, and, while some of each particular party loaded the beasts of burden, the others boiled the kettle and prepared breakfast. A few cups of tea were drunk, a few handfuls of *tsamba* eaten, and then the tent was taken down, folded, and packed. A second cannon shot gave the signal for departure.

A few of the more experienced horsemen took the lead as guides. These were followed by long files of camels, and then came the long-haired cattle, in herds of two or three hundred beasts each, under care of several herdsmen. The horsemen had no fixed place in the procession; they dashed here and there, up and down, just as their caprice suggested. The plaintive cries of the camels, the roaring of the bulls, the lowing of the cows, the neighing of the horses, the talking, bawling, laughing, singing of the travelers, the whistling of the herdsmen to the beasts of burden, and, above all, the innumerable bells tinkling from the necks of the yaks and the camels, produced together an immense, undefinable concert, which, far from wearying, seemed on the contrary to inspire everybody with fresh courage and energy.

On quitting the shore of the Blue Sea, we directed our steps towards the west, with a slight inclination southward. The first days of our march were perfect poetry: everything was just as we could have wished; the weather was magnificent, the road excellent, the water pure, the pastures rich and ample. As to brigands, we lost all thought of them. In the night it was, indeed, rather cold; but this inconvenience was easily obviated by the aid of our sheepskin coats. We asked one another what people could mean by representing this Tibet journey as something so formidable; it seemed to us impossible for any one to travel more comfortably or more agreeably. Alas! this enchantment was not of long duration.

Six days after our departure, we had to cross the Buhain-gol, a river which has its source on the slopes of the Nan Shan Mountains and throws itself into the Blue Sea. Its waters are not very deep, but, being distributed in some dozen channels, very closely to one another, they occupy altogether a breadth of more than a league. We had the misfortune to reach the first branch of the Buhain-gol long before daybreak. The water was frozen, but not thickly enough to serve as a bridge. The horses which arrived first grew alarmed and would not advance; they stopped on the bank, and gave the cattle time to come up with them. The whole caravan thus became assembled at one point, and it would be impossible to describe the disorder and confusion which prevailed in that enormous mass, amidst the darkness of night. At last several horsemen, pushing on their steeds, broke the ice, actually and figuratively, and the whole caravan followed in their train. The ice cracked in all directions, the animals stumbled about and splashed up the water, and the men shouted and vociferated; the tumult was absolutely fearful. After having traversed the first branch of the river, we had to maneuver, in the same way, over the second; and then over the third; and so on. When day broke, the whole embassy was still dabbling in the water.

At length, after infinite fatigue and infinite quaking, physical and moral, we had the delight of leaving behind us the twelve arms of the Buhain-gol and finding ourselves on dry land; but all our poetical visions had vanished, and we began to think this manner of traveling perfectly detestable. And yet everybody about us was in a state of jubilation, exclaiming that the passage of Buhain-gol had been admirably executed. Only one man had broken his legs, and only two animals had been drowned. As to the articles lost or stolen, during the protracted disorder, no one took any heed of them.

When the caravan resumed its accustomed march, it presented a truly ludicrous appearance. Men and animals were all, more or less, covered with icicles. The horses walked on, very dolefully, evidently much incommoded by their tails, which hung down all in a mass, stiff and motionless, as though they had been made of lead instead of hair. The long hair on the legs of the camels had become magnificent icicles which knocked one against the other, as the animals advanced, with harmonious discord. It was very manifest, however, that these fine ornaments were not at all to the wearers' taste, for they endeavored, from time to time, to shake them off by stamping violently on the ground. As to the long-haired oxen, they were regular caricatures:

nothing can be conceived more ludicrous than their appearance, as they slowly advanced, with legs separated to the utmost possible width in order to admit of an enormous mass of stalactites which hung from their bellies to the ground. The poor brutes had been rendered so perfectly shapeless by the agglomeration of icicles with which they were covered, that they looked as though they were preserved in sugar candy.

During the first few days of our march, we were somewhat isolated and lonely amid the multitude, being without friends or even acquaintances. However, we soon acquired companions, for there is nothing like traveling to bring men together. The companions with whom we entered into association, and beside whose tent we each day set up our own, were neither merchants, nor pilgrims, nor members of the embassy itself, nor simple travelers like ourselves: they were four lamas, who constituted a category altogether apart. Two of them were from Lhasa, one from Further Tibet, and the fourth from the kingdom of Torgut. These four young men were excellent fellows and capital traveling companions. Every day they gave us some new details of their varied adventures, which frequently helped us forget for a while the fatigues and miseries of the journey.

22

Trials and Fatigues

A PERMANENT cause of the sufferings we had
to endure was our assistant cameleer, Charadchambeul. At first this young lama appeared
to us a budding saint, but before long we found that we
had got amongst us a perfect little demon with a human
face. The following adventure opened our eyes to his character, and showed us what we should have to endure on his
account.

The day after the passage of the Buhain-gol, when we
had been traveling for a part of the night, we noticed, on
one of our camels, two great packages carefully enveloped
in wrappers, which we had not before seen. We thought,
however, that some traveler, who had not been able to find
room for them on his own pack animal, had asked Charada-
chambeul to take charge of them during the journey; and
we, accordingly, quietly pursued our way, without at the
time referring to the circumstances. When we reached our
encampment for the night, as soon as the baggage was taken
down, we saw, to our great surprise, our lama of the Ratchie
Mountains take the two packets, envelop them mysteriously
in a piece of felt, and hide them in a corner of the tent.
There was evidently something here which required explanation; and we accordingly desired Charadchambeul to inform
us what this new luggage was that we saw in the tent.

He approached and told us—in a whisper, as though fearing to be heard—that during the night Buddha had bestowed

on him a special grace, in enabling him to find on the road
a good thing; and then he added, with a knavish smile, that
at Lhasa this good thing would sell for at least ten ounces of
silver. We frowned, and insisted upon seeing this same good
thing. Charadchambeul, having first carefully closed the
door of the tent, uncovered, with infinite emotion, his pretended godsend. It consisted of two great leathern jars, full
of a sort of brandy that is distilled in the province of Kansu,
and which is sold at a high price. On these two jars were
Tibetan characters indicating the well-known name of the
proprietor. We had the charity to reject the thought that
Charadchambeul had stolen these jars during the night, and
we preferred to suppose that he had picked them up on the
road. But our assistant cameleer was a casuist of very loose
morality. He pretended that the jars belonged to him, that
Buddha had made him a present of them, and that all that
now needed to be done was carefully to conceal them, lest
the previous proprietor should discover them.

Any attempt to reason such a worthy as this into morality
and justice would have been simply lost labor and time. We
therefore emphatically declared to him that the jars were
neither ours nor his, that we would neither receive them into
our tent nor place them on our camels during the journey,
and that we had no desire whatever to arrive at Lhasa with
the character of thieves. And in order that he might labor
under no sort of misconception as to our feelings, we added
that, unless he forthwith removed the jars from our tent, we
would instantly proceed and give information of the circumstance to the proprietor. He seemed somewhat shaken by this
intimation; so, effectually to induce him to make restitution,
we advised him to carry what he had "found" to the ambassador, and request that official to return it to the owner.
The Tchanak-Kampo, we said, would not fail to be affected
by his probity, and, even if he did not give him a reward in
hand, would bear him in mind, and when we reached Lhasa
would doubtless benefit him in some way.

After animated opposition, this advice was finally adopted. Charadchambeul presented himself before the Tchanak-Kampo, and this dignitary said to him, on receiving the jars: "Thou art a good lama. A lama who has justice in his heart is acceptable to the spirits."

Charadchambeul returned perfectly furious, vehemently exclaiming that we had induced him to commit an imbecility in giving up the jars to the ambassador, who had presented him nothing in return but empty words. From that moment he vowed an implacable hatred towards us. He did his work how and when he pleased; he took delight in wasting our provisions; every day he loaded us with abuse, and in his rage he often turned upon the poor animals, and beat them about the head till he had half killed them. To discharge the wretch there, in the midst of the desert, was impossible. We were fain, therefore, to arm ourselves with patience and resignation, and to avoid irritating still more the man's untamed ferocity.

Five days after the passage of the Buhain-gol, we reached Taolai-yin-gol. This was a narrow, shallow river which we crossed without any difficulty. The caravan halted shortly afterwards near a lamasery, which had the appearance of former prosperity, but which was at the time wholly deserted. The temples and the lamas' cells, all tumbling in pieces, had become the abode of bats and of enormous rats. We heard that this Buddhist monastery, after having been besieged for three days by brigands, had been taken by them; that the greater portion of the inmates had been massacred, and the place itself plundered and demolished. From that time forth, no lama had ventured to settle in the spot. The vicinity, however, was not so entirely uninhabited as we first supposed. In walking over some rocky hills close by, we found a herd of goats and three miserable tents, concealed in a ravine. The poor inmates came out and begged for a few leaves of tea and a little *tsamba*. Their eyes were hollow, and their features pale and haggard. They knew not, they said, where to take refuge, so as to live in peace. The fear of brigands was so powerful over them that it divested them even of the courage to flee away.

On the fifteenth of November, we quitted the magnificent plains of the Koko nor and entered upon the territory of the Mongols of Tsaidam. Immediately after crossing the river of that name, we found the aspect of the country totally different. There nature becomes all of a sudden savage and sad; the soil, arid and stony, produces with difficulty a few dry, salpetrous bushes. The morose and melancholy tinge of these dismal regions seems to have had its full influence upon the character of its inhabitants, who are all evidently a prey to the spleen. They say very little, and their language is so rude and guttural that other Mongols can scarcely understand them. Mineral salt and borax abound on this arid and almost wholly pastureless soil. One digs holes two or three feet deep, and the salt collects therein, and crystallizes and purifies of itself, without the digger having to take any trouble in the matter. The borax is collected from small reservoirs, which become completely full of it. The Tibetans carry quantities of it into their own country, where they sell it to the goldsmiths, who apply it to facilitate the fusion of metals.

We stayed two days in the land of Tsaidam, feasting upon *tsamba* and some goats which the shepherds gave in exchange for some bricks of tea. The long-tailed oxen and the camels regaled themselves with the niter and salt, which they had everywhere about for the picking up. The great object with the whole caravan was to build up its strength as much as possible, with a view to the passage of the Burkhan-Buddha, a mountain noted for the pestilential vapors in which, as we were informed, it is constantly enveloped.

We started at three in the morning, and, after infinite sinuous meanderings over this hilly country, we arrived by nine o'clock at the foot of the Burkhan-Buddha. There the caravan halted for a moment, as if to gauge its strength.

Everybody measured with his eyes the steep and rugged paths of the lofty ascent; gazed with anxiety at a light, thin vapor, which we were told was the pestilential vapor in question. For a while the entire party was completely depressed and discouraged. After having taken the hygienic measures prescribed by tradition, which consist in masticating two or three cloves of garlic, we began to clamber up the side of the mountain. Before long the horses refused to carry their riders, and all, men as well as animals, advanced on foot, step by step. By degrees our faces grew pale, our hearts sick, and our legs incapable of supporting us; we threw ourselves on the ground, then rose again to make another effort; then once more prostrated ourselves, and again rose to stumble on some paces farther. In this deplorable fashion was it that we ascended the famous Burkhan-Buddha.

Heavens! what wretchedness we went through: our strength seemed exhausted, our heads turning round, our limbs dislocated. It was just like a thoroughly bad seasickness; and yet, all the while, we had to retain enough energy, not only to drag ourselves on, but moreover, to keep thrashing the animals, which lay down at every step and could hardly be got to move. One portion of the caravan, as a measure of precaution, stopped half way up the mountain, in a gully where the pestilential vapors were not so dense. The other portion of the caravan, equally as a measure of precaution, exerted their most intense efforts in order to make their way right up to the top, so as to avoid being asphyxiated by that dreadful air, so completely charged with carbonic acid. We were of the number of those who ascended the Burkhan-Buddha at one stretch. On reaching its summit, our lungs dilated at their ease. The descent of the mountain was mere child's play, and we were soon able to set up our tent far from the murderous air we had encountered on the ascent.

Burkhan-Buddha Mountain has this remarkable particularity, that the deleterious vapor for which it is noted is found only on the sides facing the east and the north; elsewhere, the air of the mountain is perfectly pure and respirable. The pestilential vapors themselves would appear to be nothing more than carbonic-acid gas. The people attached to the embassy told us that, when there is any wind, the vapors are scarcely perceptible, but that they are very dangerous when the weather is calm and serene. Carbonic-acid gas being, as the reader is aware, heavier than the atmospheric air, necessarily condenses on the surface of the ground, and remains fixed there until some great agitation of the air sets it in movement, disperses it in the atmosphere, and neutralizes its effects.

When we crossed the Burkhan-Buddha, the weather was rather calm than otherwise. We remarked that, when we were lying on the ground, respiration was much more difficult; when, on the contrary, we raised ourselves on horseback, the influence of the gas was scarcely felt. The presence of the carbonic acid rendered it very difficult to light a fire: the *argols* burned without flame and threw out great quantities of smoke. As to the manner in which the gas is formed, or as to whence it comes, we can give no sort of idea. We will merely add, for the benefit of those who are fond of seeking explanations of things in their names, that Burkhan-Buddha means "Kitchen of Buddha."

During the night we passed on the other side of the mountain, a frightful quantity of snow fell. Our companions, who had not ventured to ascend the entire mountain at once, rejoined us in the morning. They informed us that they had effected the ascent of the upper portion of the mountain easily enough, the snow having dispersed the vapor.

23
More Hardships

THE passage of the Burkhan-Buddha was but a
sort of apprenticeship. A few days later, Mount
Shugan put our strength and courage to a still
more formidable test. As the day's march would be long and
laborious, the cannon shot, our signal for departure, was
heard at one o'clock in the morning. We made our tea with
melted snow, ate a good meal of *tsamba* seasoned with
garlic cut up into small bits, and started. When the huge
caravan first set itself in motion, the sky was clear, and a
brilliant moon lit up the great carpet of snow with which
the whole country was covered. Mount Shugan is not very
steep in the direction where we approached it, and we were
able to attain the summit by sunrise.

Almost immediately afterwards, however, the sky became
thickly overcast with clouds, and the wind began to blow
with a violence which grew constantly more and more intense. The opposite side of the mountain we found so encumbered with snow that the animals were up to their girths
in it: they could only advance by a series of convulsive
efforts, which threw several of them into gulfs from which it
was impossible to extricate them, and where they accordingly perished. We marched in the very teeth of a wind so
strong and so icy that at times it absolutely choked our
respiration, and, despite our thick furs, it made us tremble
lest we should be killed with the cold. In order to avoid
the whirlwinds of snow which the wind perpetually dashed

in our faces, we followed the example of some of our fellow travelers, who mounted their horses' backs with their faces to the tails, leaving the animals to follow the guidance of their instinct. When we reached the foot of the mountain, and could use our eyes, we found that more than one face had been frozen in the descent. Poor Father Gabet, among the rest, had to deplore the temporary decease of his nose and ears. Everybody's skin was more or less chapped.

The caravan halted at the foot of Mount Shugan, and each member of it sought refuge for a while in the labyrinths of a number of adjacent ravines. We were exhausted with hunger, and our limbs were thoroughly benumbed; what we needed to restore us were a good fire, a good supper, and a good, well-warmed bed. But the Shugan is far from possessing the comfortable features of the Alps: no Buddhist monks have as yet bethought themselves of taking up their abode there for the solace and salvation of poor travelers. We were, consequently, fain to set up our tent amid the snow and go in search of what *argols* we could find.

It was a spectacle worthy of all pity to see that multitude, wandering about in all directions, and rummaging in the snow, in the hope of lighting upon some old thick bed of *argols*. For ourselves, after long and laborious research, we managed to collect just enough of the article to melt three great lumps of ice, which we extracted by aid of a hatchet from an adjacent pond. Our fire not being strong enough to boil the kettle, we had to content ourselves with steeping our *tsamba* in some tepid water, and gulping it down in order to prevent its freezing in our hands. Such was all the supper we had after our frightful day's journey! We then rolled ourselves up in our goatskins and blankets, and, crouching in a corner of the tent, awaited the cannon shot that was to summon us next morning.

We left, in this picturesque and enchanting encampment, the Tartar and Chinese soldiers who had escorted us since our departure from Koko nor. They were no longer to extend to us their generous protection, and the embassy would thereafter have to rely upon its own internal resources. As we have already stated, this great body of two thousand men was completely armed, and every one, without exception, had announced that he was prepared to show himself, upon occasion, a good soldier. But somehow or other the martial and valorous air of the caravan had become cingularly modified since the passage of the Burkhan-Buddha. Nobody sang now, nobody joked, nobody laughed, nobody pranced about on his horse; everybody was dull and silent; the mustaches, which heretofore had been so fiercely turned up, were now humbly veiled beneath the lambskins with which all our faces were covered up to the eyes. All our gallant soldiers had made up their lances, sabers, bows and arrows, into bundles, which were packed upon their animals. For that matter, the fear of being killed by the brigands scarcely occurred now to any one: the point was to avoid being killed by the cold.

It was on Mount Shugan that the long train of our miseries really began. The snow, the wind, and the cold there set to work upon us, with a fury which daily increased. The deserts of Tibet are certainly the most frightful country that it is possible to conceive. The ground continues to rise, vegetation diminishes as the traveler advances, and the cold grows more and more intense. Death now hovered over the unfortunate caravan. The want of water and of pasturage soon destroyed the strength of our animals. Each day we had to abandon beasts of burden that could drag themselves on no farther. The men's turn came somewhat later. The road was dismal. For several days we traveled through what seemed the excavations of a great cemetery. Human bones and the carcasses of animals, presenting themselves at every step, seemed to warn us that, in this fatal region, amidst this savage nature, the caravans which had preceded us had fared no better than we.

To complete our misery, Father Gabet fell ill, his health

abandoning him just at the moment when the frightful difficulties of the route called for redoubled energy and courage. The excessive cold he had undergone on the passage of Mount Shugan had entirely broken down his strength. To regain his previous vigor, he needed repose, tonic drinks, and substantial nourishment; whereas, all we had to give him was barley meal, and tea made with snow water. Moreover, notwithstanding his extreme weakness, he had every day to ride on horseback, and to struggle against an iron climate. And we had two months more of this traveling before us, in the depth of winter. Our prospect was, indeed, somber!

Towards the commencement of September, we arrived in sight of the Bayan Kara, a famous chain of mountains, extending from southeast to northwest, between the Hwang-Ho and the Chin-kiang. These two great rivers, after running a parallel course on either side of the Bayan Kara, then separate and take opposite directions, the one towards the north, the other towards the south. After a thousand capricious meanderings in Tartary and Tibet, they both enter the Chinese Empire; after having watered it from west to east, they approach each other, towards their mouths, and fall into the Yellow River. They lay on our left, and a couple of days' journey would have enabled us to visit them; but this was by no means the season for pleasure trips. We had no fancy for a tourist's excursion to the sources of the Yellow River; how to cross the Bayan Kara was ample occupation for our thoughts.

From its foot to its summit, the mountain was completely enveloped in a thick coat of snow. Before undertaking the ascent, the principal members of the embassy held a council. The question was not whether they should cross the mountain—if they desired to reach Lhasa, the passage of the mountain was an essential preliminary. Nor was it the question, whether they should await the melting of the snow. The point was simply whether it would be more advantageous to ascend the mountain at once or to wait till next day. The fear of avalanches filled every one's mind, and we should all have liked to have an assurance against the wind. After the example of all the councils in the world, the council of the Tibetan embassy was soon divided into two parties, the one contending that it would be better to start forthwith, the other insisting that we ought, by all means, to wait till the morrow.

To extricate themselves from this embarrassment, they had recourse to the lamas, who had the reputation of being diviners. But this expedient did not combine all minds in unity. Among the diviners there were some who declared that this day would be calm, but that the next day would have a terrible wind; and there were others who announced an exactly contrary opinion. The caravan thus became divided into two camps, that of movement and that of non-movement. It will at once be understood that, in our character of French citizens, we instinctively placed ourselves in the ranks of those who desired to advance and to have done with this villainous mountain as soon as possible.

It appeared to us, moreover, that reason was altogether on our side. The weather just then was perfectly calm, but we knew not what it might be on the morrow. Our party, therefore, proceeded to scale these mountains of snow, sometimes on horseback, but more frequently on foot. In the latter case we made our animals precede us, and we hung on to their tails, a mode of ascending mountains which is less fatiguing than one would imagine. Father Gabet suffered dreadfully, but God, in His infinite goodness, gave us strength and energy enough to reach the other side. The weather was calm throughout, and we were assailed by no avalanche whatever.

24
Sky High Road

NEXT morning, at daybreak, the group who had remained behind advanced and crossed the mountain with entire success. As we had had the politeness to wait for them, they joined us, and we entered together a valley where the temperature was comparatively mild. The excellence of the pasturage induced the caravan to take a day's rest there. A deep lake, in the ice of which we dug wells, supplied us with abundance of water. We had plenty of fuel, too, for, as the embassies and pilgrimages were in the habit of halting in the valley after the passage of the Bayan Kara, one is always sure to find plenty of argols there. We all kept up great fires throughout our stay, burning all the burnable things we could find, without the smallest consideration for our successors. Our fifteen thousand long-haired oxen would supply the deficit.

When we quitted the great valley of Bayan Kara, we set up our tents on the banks of the Murus, or, as the Tibetans call it, River of the Lord. Towards its source, this magnificent river bears the name of Tortuous; further on it is called River of Golden Sand; and arrived in the province of Szechwan, it becomes the famous Yangtze.

As we were crossing the Tortuous River, on the ice, a singular spectacle presented itself. We had previously, from our encampment, observed dark, shapeless masses ranged across this great river; and it was not until we came quite close to these fantastic islets that we could at all make head or tail of them. Then we found out that they were neither more nor less than upwards of fifty wild cattle, absolutely encrusted in the ice. They had no doubt attempted to swim across the river, at the precise moment of the congealing of the waters, and had been so hemmed in by the flakes as to be unable to extricate themselves. Their fine heads, surmounted with great horns, were still above the surface; the rest of the bodies were enclosed by the ice, and this was so transparent as to give a full view of the form and position of the unlucky animals, which looked as though they were still swimming.

Some days after the passage of the Murus, the caravan began to break up; those who had camels went on ahead, refusing to be any longer delayed by the slow progress of the long-haired oxen. Besides, the nature of the country no longer permitted so large a body to encamp on one spot. The pasturages had become so scarce and meager that the animals of the caravan could not travel all together without the danger of starving. We joined the camel party, and soon left behind us the long-haired oxen. The camel party itself was before long fain to subdivide; and, the unity once broken, a crowd of petty chiefs of caravans arose who did not always agree, either as to the place of encampment or the hour of departure.

We were imperceptibly attaining the highest point of Upper Asia, when a terrible north wind which lasted fifteen days, combined with the fearful severity of the temperature, and menaced us with destruction. The weather was always clear; but the cold was so intense that even at midday we scarcely felt the influence of the sun's rays, and we still had to seek shelter from the wind. During the rest of the day, and more especially during the night, we were in constant apprehension of dying with cold. Everybody's face and hands were frostbitten.

To give something like an idea of this cold—the reality of which, however, can never be appreciated except by those

who have felt it—it may suffice to mention a circumstance
which seemed to us rather striking. Every morning, before
proceeding on our journey, we ate a meal; and then we did
not eat again until the evening after we had encamped. As
tsamba is not a very toothsome affair, we could not get
down, at a time, as much as was required for our nourishment during the day; so we used to make three or four balls
of it, with our tea, and keep these in reserve, to be eaten
from time to time on our road. The hot paste was wrapped
in a piece of hot linen, and then deposited in our breasts.
Over it were all our clothes; to wit, a thick robe of sheepskin, then a lambskin jacket, then a short foxskin cloak, and
then a great wool overall. Now, upon every one of the fifteen
days in question, our *tsamba* cakes were always frozen; when
we took them out, they were merely so many balls of ice.
Notwithstanding, we were fain to devour them, at the risk
of breaking our teeth, in order to avoid the greater risk of
starvation.

The animals, overcome with fatigue and privation, had
infinite difficulty in resisting the intensity of the cold. The
mules and horses, being less vigorous than the camels and
long-haired oxen, required especial attention. We were
obliged to pack them in great pieces of carpet, carefully
fastened round the bodies. The heads were enveloped in
rolls of camel's hair. Under any other circumstances this
singular costume would have excited our hilarity, but just
then we were in no laughing mood. Despite all these precautions, the animals of the caravans were decimated by
death.

The numerous rivers that we had to cross upon the ice
were another source of inconceivable misery and fatigue.
Camels are so awkward, and their walk is so uncouth and
heavy, that, in order to facilitate their passage, we were
compelled to make a path for them across each river, either
by strewing sand and dust, or by breaking the first coat of
ice with our hatchets. After this we had to take the brutes,

one by one, and guide them carefully over the path thus traced out. If they had the ill luck to stumble or slip, it was all over with them; down they threw themselves on the ice, and only with the utmost labor could they be got up again. We had first to take off their baggage, then to drag them with ropes to the bank, and then to stretch a carpet on which they might be induced to rise. Sometimes all this labor was lost: we might beat the obstinate animals, pull them, kick them; not an effort would they make to get on their legs. In such cases, the only course was to leave them where they lay, for it was clearly impossible to wait, in those hideous localities, until the beasts should choose to rise.

All these combined miseries ended in casting the poor travelers into a depression bordering on despair. To the mortality of the animals was now added that of the men who, hopelessly overpowered by the cold, were abandoned, yet living, on the road. One day, when the exhaustion of our animals had compelled us to relax our march, so that we were somewhat behind the main body, we perceived a traveler sitting on a great stone, his head bent forward on his chest, his arms pressed against his sides, and his whole frame motionless as a statue. We called to him several times, but he made no reply, and did not even indicate, by the slightest movement, that he heard us. "How absurd," said we to each other, "for a man to loiter in this way in such dreadful weather! The wretched fellow will assuredly die of cold."

We called to him once more, but he remained silent and motionless as before. We dismounted, went up to him, and recognized in him a young Mongol lama, who had often paid us a visit in our tent. His face was exactly like wax, and his eyes, half-opened, had a glassy appearance; icicles hung from his nostrils and from the corners of his mouth. We spoke to him, but obtained no answer; and for a moment we thought him dead. Presently, however, he opened his eyes, and fixed them upon us with a horrible expression of stupefaction: the poor creature was freezing, and we comprehended at once that he had been abandoned by his companions. It seemed to us so frightful to leave a man to die, without making an effort to save him, that we did not hesitate to take him with us.

We took him from the stone on which he had been placed, enveloped him in a covering, seated him upon Samdadchiemba's little mule, and thus brought him to the encampment. When we had set up our tent, we went to visit the companions of this poor young man. Upon our informing them what we had done, they prostrated themselves in token of thanks and said that we were people of excellent hearts, but assured us that we had given ourselves much labor in vain, for the case was beyond cure. "He is frozen," said they, "and nothing can prevent the cold from getting to his heart."

We ourselves did not share in this despairing view of the case, and returned to our tent, accompanied by one of the patient's companions, to see what further could be done. When we reached our temporary home, the young lama was dead.

More than forty men of the caravan were abandoned still living, in the desert, without the slightest possibility of our aiding them. They were carried on horseback and on camelback so long as any hope remained; but when they could no longer eat, or speak, or hold themselves up, they were left on the wayside. The general body of the caravan could not stay to nurse them in a barren desert, where there was hourly danger of wild beasts, of robbers, and, worst of all, of a deficiency of food. Yet it was a fearful spectacle—those dying men abandoned on the road! As a last token of sympathy, we placed beside each a wooden cup and a small bag of barley meal, and then the caravan mournfully proceeded on its way. As soon as the last straggler had passed on, the crows and vultures that incessantly hovered above the caravan would pounce down upon the unhappy creatures,

who retained just enough of life to feel themselves torn and
mangled by these birds of prey.

The north wind greatly aggravated Father Gabet's malady.
From day to day his condition grew more alarming. His
extreme weakness would not permit him to walk, and, as
he was thus precluded from warming himself by means of
a little exercise, his feet, hands, and face were completely
frozen. His lips became livid, and his eyes almost extinct;
by and by he was not able to support himself on horseback. Our only remedy was to wrap him in blankets, to
pack him upon a camel, and to leave the rest to the merci-
ful goodness of Divine Providence.

25
Robbers

ONE day, as we were following the windings of a valley, our hearts oppressed with sad thoughts, all of a sudden we perceived two horsemen make their appearance on the ridge of an adjacent hill. At this time we were traveling in the company of a small party of Tibetan merchants who, like ourselves, had allowed the main body of the caravan to precede them in order to save their camels the fatigue of a too-hurried march. "Tsong-Kaba!" cried the Tibetans. "See, there are horsemen yonder, yet we are in the desert, and everyone knows that there are not even shepherds in this locality."

They had scarcely uttered these words, when a number of other horsemen appeared at different points on the hills and, to our extreme alarm, dashed down towards us at a gallop. What could these horsemen be doing in so barren a region? What could they want with us? The case was clear: we had fallen into the hands of thieves! Their appearance, as they approached, was anything but reassuring. A carbine slung at the saddlebow, two long sabers in the girdle, thick black hair falling in disorder over the shoulders, glaring eyes, and a wolf's skin stuck on the head by the way of cap: such was the portrait of each of the gentlemen who now favored us with their company. There were twenty-seven of them, while we numbered only eighteen, and of these eighteen all were by no means practiced warriors. However, both armies alighted, and a valorous Tibetan of our

136

party advanced to parley with the chief of the brigands, who was distinguished from his men by two red pennants which floated from his saddle back.

After a long and somewhat animated conversation, "Who is that man?" asked the chief of the robbers, pointing to Father Gabet, who, fastened upon his camel, was the only person who had not alighted.

"He is a Grand Lama of the western sky," replied the Tibetan merchant; "the power of his prayers is infinite."

The bandit chief raised his clasped hands to his forehead, in token of respect, and looked at Father Gabet, who, with his frozen face, and his singular envelope of many-colored wrappings, was by no means unlike those alarming idols that we see in pagan temples. After contemplating for a while the famous lama of the western sky, the brigand addressed some further words, in an undertone, to the Tibetan merchant. Then he made a sign to his companions, and they all jumped into their saddles, set off at a gallop, and soon disappeared behind the mountains.

"Do not let us go any farther today," said the Tibetan merchant, "but set up our tents where we are. These men are robbers, but they have lofty and generous souls; when they see that we place ourselves without fear in their hands, they will not attack us. Besides," added he, "I believe they hold in much awe the power of the lamas of the western sky."

We adopted the counsel of the Tibetan merchant and proceeded to encamp. The tents were scarcely set up, however, when the bandits reappeared on the crest of the mountain, and once more galloped down upon us with their habitual impetuosity. The chief alone entered the encampment, his men awaiting him at a short distance outside. He addressed the Tibetan who had previously conversed with him.

"I have come," said he, "for an explanation of a point that I don't at all understand. You know that we are encamped on the other side of the mountain, yet you venture to set up your tents here, close by us. How many men, then, have you in your company?"

"We are only eighteen. You, I believe, are twenty-seven in number; but brave men never run away."

"You'll fight, then?"

"If there were not several invalids amongst us, I would answer, 'Yes'; for I have already shown you robbers that I am not afraid of you."

"Have you fought us before? When was it? What's your name?"

"I fought five years ago at the affair of the Tchanak-Kampo, and here's a little souvenir of it"; and, throwing back the sleeve of his right arm, he showed the scar of a great saber cut. The brigand laughed, and again requested his interlocutor's name.

"I am called Rala-Tchembe," said the merchant; "you ought to know the name."

"Yes, all of us know it. It is the name of a brave man." So saying, he dismounted, and taking a saber from his girdle, presented it to the Tibetan. "Here," said he, "accept this saber; 'tis the best I have. We have fought enough; in future, when we meet, it shall be as brothers."

The Tibetan received the brigand's present and gave him, in return, a handsome bow and quiver which he had bought at Peking.

The robbers who had remained outside the camp, upon seeing their chief fraternize with the chief of the caravan, dismounted, fastened their horses to each other, two and two, by the bridles, and came to drink a friendly cup of tea with the travelers, who now at last began to breathe freely. All these brigands were extremely affable. They asked us various questions about the Tartar-Khalkhas, whom, they said, they were particularly anxious to see for the reason that, in the preceding year, these warriors had killed three of their companions, and they were eager to avenge them. We

had a little chat about politics, too. The brigands affirmed
that they were warm friends of the Grand Lama and irre-
concilable enemies of the Emperor of China. On this account they seldom failed to pillage the embassy on its way
to Peking, because the Emperor was unworthy to receive
gifts from the Grand Lama; but ordinarily they respected it
on its return, because it was altogether fitting that the Emperor should send gifts to the Grand Lama.

After having done honor to the tea and *tsamba* of the
caravan, the brigands wished us a good journey and returned
to their own encampment. All these fraternal manifestations
did not prevent our sleeping with one eye open; our repose,
however, was not disturbed, and in the morning we resumed
our way in peace. Of the many thousands of pilgrims who
have performed the journey to Lhasa, there are very few who
can boast of having had so close a view of the robbers, at so
small a cost.

26
Over the Top

W E had escaped one great danger; but, we were informed, another awaited us, far more formidable in its character though different in kind. We were beginning to ascend the vast chain of the Tangla Mountains. On the plateau of these, our traveling companions assured us, the invalids would die, and those who were now well would become invalids, with but a small chance of living. The death of Father Gabet was considered quite a matter of certainty.

After six days' laborious ascent of several mountains, which rose, one above another, like tiers in a natural amphitheater, we at length reached the famous plateau—the most elevated point, perhaps, on the earth's surface. The snow there appeared to have identified itself with the soil. It cracked beneath our feet, but the feet left scarcely any impression upon it. The only vegetation consisted of occasional tufts of a low, sharp-pointed, smooth grass, woody within and as hard as iron, but not brittle; so that it might very well be used for mattress needles. The animals were, however, so famished that they were fain to attack even this atrocious forage, which actually cracked between their teeth and could be gathered only by vigorous efforts and at the cost of infinite lip bleeding.

From the brow of this magnificent plateau we could see below us the peaks and needles of numerous ridges, the rami-

fications of which were lost in the horizon. We had never
witnessed anything at all comparable to this grand, this
gigantic spectacle. During the twelve days that we were
journeying along the heights of Tangla, we enjoyed fine
weather; the air was calm, and it pleased God to bless us each
day with a warm, genial sunshine that materially modified
the ordinary coldness of the atmosphere. Still, the air, excessively rarified at that enormous altitude, was very piercing, and monstrous vultures, which followed the track of the
caravan, were daily provided with a number of dead
bodies.

The small caravan of missioners itself paid its tribute to
death; but, happily, that tribute was only in the shape of our
little black mule, which we abandoned with regret but at
the same time with resignation. The dismal prophecy that
had been announced with reference to Father Gabet was
not fulfilled. The mountains which were to have been fatal
to him proved, on the contrary, highly favorable, restoring
to him, by degrees, health and strength. This blessing, almost unexpected by us, even at the hands of the God of
Mercy, made us forget all our past miseries. We regained all
our courage, and firmly entertained the hope that the Almighty would permit us to accomplish our journey.

The descent of Tangla, though long in duration, was rapid
in itself. Throughout four whole days we were going down,
as it seemed, a gigantic staircase, each step of which consisted of a mountain. At the bottom we found some hot
springs, of an extremely magnificent description. Amongst
huge rocks are a great number of reservoirs, hollowed out
by the hand of nature, in which the water boils and bubbles,
as in a vast cauldron over a fierce fire. Sometimes the active
fluid escapes through the fissures of the rocks, and leaps in
all directions by a thousand capricious jets. Every now and
then the ebullition, in particular reservoirs, grows so furious
that tall columns of water rise into the air, as though impelled by some tremendous pump. Above these springs,

thick vapors, collecting in the air, condense into white clouds.

The water of these hot springs is sulphurous. After bubbling and dashing about in its huge granite reservoirs, it boils over and, quitting the rocks, which had seemed to wish to keep it captive, pours down by various currents into a small valley below. There it forms a large stream flowing over a bed of flint, yellow as gold. These boiling waters do not long preserve their fluidity. The extreme rigor of the atmosphere cools them so rapidly that, within a mile and a half from its source, the stream they have formed is almost frozen through. These hot springs are of frequent occurrence in the mountains of Tibet; and the lama physicians, who attribute to them considerable medicinal virtue, constantly prescribe their use, both internally and externally.

From the Tangla Mountains to Lhasa, the ground constantly declines. As the traveler descends, the intensity of the cold diminishes, and the earth becomes clothed with more vigorous and more varied vegetation. One evening we encamped in a large plain, where the pasturage was marvelously abundant. As our cattle had been for some time past on very short rations indeed, we determined to give them the full benefit of the present opportunity, and to remain where we were for two days.

Next morning, when we were quietly preparing our tea, we perceived in the distance a troop of horsemen galloping towards our encampment at full speed. The sight seemed to freeze the very blood in our veins: we stood for a moment perfectly petrified. After the first moment of stupor, we rushed out of our tent. "Robbers! Robbers!" cried we. "Here's a great body of bandits advancing against us."

The Tibetan merchants, who were boiling their tea and mixing their *tsamba*, laughed at our alarm, and told us to sit down quite at our ease. "Take breakfast with us," said they. "There are no robbers to fear here; the horsemen you see yonder are friends. We are now entering upon an inhabited

country. Behind the hill there, to the right, are a number of
black tents, and the horsemen, whom you take to be robbers,
are shepherds."

These words restored our equanimity, and with our equanimity returned our appetite, so that we were very happy
to accept the invitation to breakfast. We had scarcely taken
up a cup of buttered tea before the horsemen made their
appearance at the door of the tent. Far from being brigands,
they were worthy fellows who came to sell us butter and
fresh meat; their saddles were regular butchers' stalls hung
with joints of mutton and venison, which rested on the sides
of their horses. We purchased eight legs of mutton, which,
being frozen, were easily susceptible of transport. They cost
us an old pair of Peking boots, a Peking steel, and the saddle
of our defunct mule, which luckily could also boast of
Peking origin.

Everything coming from Peking is highly prized by the
Tibetans, more especially by that portion of the population
which has not advanced beyond the pastoral and nomadic
life. The merchants who accompany caravans take care,
accordingly, to label every package "Goods from Peking."
Snuff is especially an object earnestly sought for among the
Tibetans: all the shepherds asked us whether we had snuff
from Peking. Father Huc, who was the only snuff-taker of
our party, had formerly possessed a quantity of the precious
commodity, but it had all been used, and for the last eight
days he had been reduced to the necessity of filling his snuff-
box and his nose with a frightful mixture of dust and ashes.
Those who are devotees of snuff will at once comprehend
all the horrors to poor Father Huc of this deplorable position.

Condemned for the two last months to live upon barley
meal moistened with tea, we found that the mere sight of
our legs of mutton seemed to fortify our stomachs and in-
vigorate our emaciated limbs. The remainder of the day
was occupied in culinary preparations. By way of condi-

ment and seasoning, we had only a little garlic, and that little was so frozen and dried that it was almost imperceptible in its shell. We peeled, however, all we had, and stuck it into two legs of mutton, which we set to boil in our great cauldron. The argols, which abounded in this blessed plain, supplied ample materials for cooking our inestimable supper.

The sun was just setting, and Samdadchiemba, who had been inspecting one of the legs of mutton with his thumbnail, had triumphantly announced that the mutton was boiled to a bubble, when we heard in all directions the frightening cry, "Fire! fire!" At one bound we were outside our tent, where we found that the flame, which had caught some dry grass in the interior of the encampment and threatened to assail also our linen tents, was spreading about, in all directions, with fearful rapidity.

All the travelers, armed with their felt carpets, were endeavoring to stifle the flame, or at all events to keep it from reaching the tents, and in this latter effort they were quite successful. The fire, repulsed on every side, forced an issue from the encampment and rushed out into the desert. There, driven by the wind, it spread over the pasturages, which it devoured as it went. We thought that we had nothing further to fear; but the cry, "Save the camels! Save the camels!" at once reminded us how little we knew of a conflagration in the desert.

We then saw that the camels stolidly awaited the flame, instead of fleeing from it as the horses and oxen did. We therefore hastened to the succor of our own beasts, which, at the moment, seemed tolerably remote from the flame. The flame, however, reached them as soon as we did, and at once surrounded us and them. It was to no purpose we pushed and beat the stupid brutes; not an inch would they stir; but there they stood, phlegmatically gaping at us with an air that seemed to ask us what right we had to come and interrupt them at their meals. We really felt as if we could have killed the impractical beasts. The fire consumed so rapidly the grass it encountered, that it soon assailed the camels and caught their long, thick hair; and it was only with the utmost exertion that, by the aid of the felt carpets we had brought with us, we extinguished the flame upon their bodies. We got three of them out of the fire, with the ends of their hair singed, but the fourth was reduced to a deplorable condition. Not a bristle remained on its entire body; the whole coat of hair was burned down to the skin, and the skin itself was terribly charred.

The extent of pasturage consumed by the flame was about a mile and a quarter long by three quarters of a mile broad. The Tibetans were in ecstasies at their good fortune in having the progress of the conflagration so soon stayed, and we fully participated in their joy after we had learned the full extent of the evil with which we had been menaced. We were informed that, if the fire had continued much longer, it would have reached the black tents, in which case the shepherds would have pursued and massacred us. Nothing can equal the fury of these poor children of the desert when they find the pastures, which are their only resource, reduced to ashes, no matter whether by malice or by mischance. It is much the same thing to them as destroying their herds.

When we resumed our journey, the broiled camel was not yet dead, but it was altogether incapable of service. The three others were obliged to yield to circumstances, and to share among them the portion of baggage which their unlucky traveling companion had hitherto borne. However, the burdens of all of them had very materially diminished in weight since our departure from Koko nor: our sacks of meal had become little better than sacks of emptiness; so that, after descending the Tangla Mountains, we had been compelled to put ourselves upon an allowance of two cups of *tsamba* each, a day. Before our departure we had made a fair calculation of our reasonable wants, but no such calculation could cover the waste committed upon our provender by our two cameleers—by the one through indifference and stupidity, by the other through malice and knavery. Fortunately we were soon approaching a large Tibetan station, where we should find the means of renewing our stores.

27
Civilization Again

FOR several days we had followed a long series of valleys, in which we saw, from time to time, black tents and great herds of yaks. At last we encamped beside a large Tibetan village, on the banks of the river Nazu-zir—which signifies "Black Waters." The village of Nazu-zir is the first Tibetan station of any importance on this route to Lhasa. The village consists of mud houses and a number of black tents. The inhabitants do not cultivate the ground. Although they always live on the same spot, they are shepherds like the nomadic tribes, and occupy themselves solely with the breeding of cattle.

We were informed that, at some very remote period, a king of Koko nor made war upon the Tibetans and, when he had subjugated them to a large extent, gave their district of Nazu-zir to the soldiers whom he had brought with him. Though these Tartars have become fused with the Tibetans, one may still observe among the black tents a certain number of Mongol huts. This event may also serve to explain the origin of a number of Mongol expressions which are used in the country and pass as Tibetan idiom.

The caravans which repair to Lhasa are obliged to remain several days at Nazu-zir, in order to arrange a fresh system of conveyance; for the difficulties of an extremely rocky road do not permit camels to proceed further. Our first business, therefore, was to sell our animals; but they were so wretchedly worn that no buyer would look at them. At last a sort of veterinary surgeon, who, doubtless, had some recipe for restoring their strength and looks, made us an offer; and we sold him the three for fifteen ounces of silver, throwing the grilled one into the bargain. These fifteen ounces of silver just sufficed to pay the hire of six long-haired oxen, to carry our baggage to Lhasa.

A second operation was to discharge the lama of the Ratchie Mountains. After having settled with him on very liberal terms, we told him that, if he proposed to visit Lhasa, he must find some other companions, for he might consider himself wholly freed from the engagements which he had contracted with us. So at last we got rid of this rascal, whose misconduct had fully doubled the trouble and misery that we had experienced on the way in his company.

Our conscience imposes upon us the duty of here warning persons whom any circumstances may lead to Nazu-zir to be carefully on their guard there against thieves. The inhabitants of this Tibetan village are remarkable for their peculations: in the most shameful manner, they rob every caravan that comes to the place. At night they creep into the travelers' tents, and carry off whatever they can lay hands upon; and in broad day itself they exercise their deplorable ingenuity in this line with a coolness, a presence of mind, and an ability that might arouse envy in the most distinguished Parisian thieves.

After having laid in a supply of butter, *tsamba*, and legs of mutton, we proceeded on our way to Lhasa, from which we were distant now only fifteen days' march. Our traveling companions were some Mongols of the kingdom of Kharachin, who were repairing in pilgrimage to the Eternal Sanctuary, as the Tartars called Lhasa, and who had with them their Grand *Chaberon*; that is to say, a "Living Buddha," the superior of the lamasery. The *chaberon* was a young man of eighteen, whose manners were agreeable and gentlemanly, and whose face, full of ingenuous candor, contrasted singularly with the part which he was constrained habitually

to enact. At the age of five, he had been declared Buddha
and Grand Lama of the Buddhists of Kharachin, and he
was now about to pass a few years in one of the great lamaseries of Lhasa, in the study of prayers and other knowledge
befitting his dignity. A brother of the King of Kharachin
and several lamas of quality were in attendance to escort and
wait upon him.

The title of Living Buddha seemed to be a dead weight
upon this poor young man. It was quite manifest that he
would very much have liked to laugh and chat and frolic
about at his ease; and that, en route, it would have been far
more agreeable to him to have dashed about on his horse,
whither he fancied, than to ride, as he did, solemnly between two horsemen who, out of their extreme respect,
never once quitted his side. Again, when they had reached
an encampment, instead of remaining eternally squatted on
cushions in a corner of his tent, imitating the idols in the
lamasery, he would have liked to ramble about the desert,
taking part in the occupations of nomadic life. But he was
permitted to do nothing of the sort; his business was to be
Buddha, and to concern himself in no degree with matters
which appertained to mere mortals.

The young *chaberon* derived no small pleasure from an
occasional chat in our tent; there, at all events, he was able
to lay aside, for a time, his official divinity and to belong
to mankind. He heard with great interest what we told
him about the men and things of Europe; and he ques-
tioned us, with much ingenuity, respecting our religion,
which evidently appeared to him a very fine one. When we
asked him whether it would not be better to be a worshiper
of God than a *chaberon,* he replied that he could not say.
He did not at all like us to interrogate him respecting his
interior life and his continual incarnations: he would blush
when any such questions were put to him, and would always
put an end to the conversation by saying that the subject
was painful to him. The simple fact was that the poor lad

found himself involved in a sort of religious labyrinth, the meanderings of which were completely unknown to him.

The road which leads from Nazu-zir to Lhasa is, in general, rocky and very difficult, and when it attains the chain of the Koïran Mountains it becomes fatiguing in the highest degree. Yet as the traveler advances, his heart grows lighter and lighter, at finding himself in a more and more populous country. The black tents that speckle the background of the landscape, the numerous parties of pilgrims repairing to Lhasa, the infinite inscriptions engraved on the stones erected on each side of the way, the small caravans of long-haired oxen met at intervals—all contribute to alleviate the fatigues of the journey.

When one comes within a few days' march of Lhasa, the exclusively nomadic character of the Tibetans begins to disappear. A few cultivated fields adorn the desert; houses gradually take the place of the black tents. At length the shepherds vanish altogether, and the traveler finds himself amidst an agricultural people.

On the fifteenth day after our departure from Nazu-zir, we arrived at Pampu. This settlement, on account of its proximity to Lhasa, is regarded by the pilgrims as the vestibule of the holy city. Pampu is a fine plain watered by a broad river, a portion of which, diverted in canals, diffuses fertility all around. There is no village, properly so called; but one sees, in all directions, large farmhouses with handsome terraces in front, and beautifully white with lime wash. Each is surrounded with tall trees, and surmounted with a little tower in the form of a pigeon house, whence float banners of various colors, covered with Tibetan inscriptions. After we had traveled for more than three months through hideous deserts, where the only living creatures one meets are brigands and wild beasts, the plain of Pampu seemed to us the most charming spot in the world.

Our long and painful journeying had so nearly reduced us to the savage state that anything in the shape of civilization struck us as absolutely marvelous. We were in ecstasy at everything: a house, a tree, a plow, a furrow in the plowed field—the slightest object seemed to us worthy of attention. That, however, which most forcibly impressed us was the prodigious height of the temperature which we noticed in this cultivated plain. Although it was now the end of January, the river and its canals were merely edged with a thin coat of ice, and scarcely any of the people wore furs.

At Pampu, our caravan had to undergo another transformation. Generally speaking, the long-haired oxen are here replaced by donkeys, small in size, but very robust, and accustomed to carrying baggage. The difficulty of procuring a sufficient number of these donkeys to convey the baggage of the Kharachin lamas rendered it necessary for us to remain two days at Pampu. We availed ourselves of the opportunity to improve our appearance as well as we could. Our hair and beards were so thick, our faces so blackened with the smoke of the tent, so furrowed with the cold, so worn, so deplorable, that, when we had here the means of looking at ourselves in a glass, we were ready to weep with compassion at our appearance. Our costumes were perfectly in harmony with our persons.

The people of Pampu are for the most part in very easy circumstances, and they are always gay and frolicsome accordingly. Every evening they assemble in front of the different farms, where men, women, and children dance to the accompaniment of their own voices. On the termination of the dance, the farmer regales the company with a sort of sharp drink, made with fermented barley. We thought that this drink, if mixed with hops, would be very like our beer.

After a two days' search through all the farms of the neighborhood, the donkey caravan was organized, and we went on our way. Between us and Lhasa there was only a mountain, but this mountain was, past contradiction, the most rugged and toilsome that we had yet encountered. The Tibetans and Mongols ascend it with great enthusiasm, for it is understood amongst them that whoever attains its summit attains, *ipso facto*, a remission of all his sins. It is certain, at all events, that whoever attains the summit has undergone on his way a most severe penance; but whether that penance is adequate to the remission of sins is another question altogether. We started out at one o'clock in the morning, yet it was not till ten in the forenoon that we reached the summit. We had to walk nearly the whole distance, since it was so difficult to retain one's seat on horseback along the rugged and rocky path.

28

Lhasa!

THE sun was nearly setting when, issuing from the last of the infinite meanderings of the mountain, we found ourselves in a vast plain and saw on our right Lhasa, the famous metropolis of the Buddhist world. The multitude of aged trees which surround the city with a verdant wall; the tall white houses, with their flat roofs and their towers; the numerous temples with their gilt roofs; the Buddha-La, above which rises the palace of the Grand Lama—all these features communicate to Lhasa a majestic and imposing aspect.

At the entrance of the town, some Mongols with whom we had formed an acquaintance on the road, and who had preceded us by several days, met us and invited us to accompany them to lodgings which they had been friendly enough to prepare for us. It was now January 29, 1846; and it was eighteen months since we had left the Valley of Black Waters.

The morning after our arrival at Lhasa, we engaged a Tibetan guide and visited the various quarters of the city in search of a lodging. The houses at Lhasa are for the most part several stories high, and the roof of each terminates in a terrace, slightly sloped in order to carry off the water. The houses are whitewashed all over, except for the borders around doors and windows, which are painted red or yellow. Reformed Buddhists are so fond of these two colors, which are, so to speak, sacred in their eyes, that they especially name them "Lamaistic colors." The people of Lhasa are in the habit of painting their homes once a year, so that the houses are always perfectly clean on the exterior, and seem, in fact, just built; but the interiors are by no means in harmony with the fine outsides. The rooms are dirty, smoky, stinking, and encumbered with all sorts of utensils and furniture, thrown about in most disgusting confusion. In a word, the Tibetan habitations are literally whited sepulchers —perfect pictures of Buddhism and all other false religions, which carefully cover, with certain dogmatic truths and certain moral principles, the corruption and falsehood within.

After a long search we selected two rooms, in a large house that contained in all fifty lodgers. Our humble abode was at the top of the house, and to reach it we had to ascend twenty-six wooden stairs. These were without railing, and so steep and narrow that, in order to prevent the disagreeable accident of breaking our necks, we always found it prudent to use our hands as well as our feet. Our suite of apartments consisted of one great square room and a little corridor which we called a closet. The larger room was lighted from above by a small round skylight, and at the northeast by a narrow window, provided with three thick wooden bars. The skylight served a variety of purposes: first, it gave entrance to the light, the wind, the rain, and the snow: and secondly, it gave issue to the smoke from our fire. To protect themselves from the winter's cold, the Tibetans place in the center of a room a small vessel of glazed earth, in which they burn *argols*. As this combustible is extremely addicted to diffusing considerably more smoke than heat, those who desire to warm themselves find it of infinite advantage to have a hole in the ceiling, which enables them to light a fire without incurring the risk of being stifled by the smoke. One does, indeed, undergo the small inconvenience of receiving, from time to time, a fall of snow or rain on one's back; but those who have followed the nomadic life are not disturbed by such trifles.

The furniture of our larger apartment consisted of two goatskins spread on the floor at the right and left of the fire dish; of two saddles, our traveling tent, some old pairs of boots, two dilapidated trunks, three ragged robes hanging from nails in the wall, our night things rolled together in a bundle, and a supply of *argols* in the corner. We were thus placed at once on the full level of Tibetan civilization. The closet, in which stood a large brick stove, served us for kitchen and pantry, and there we installed Samdadchiemba, who, having resigned his office of cameleer, now fulfilled the functions of cook, steward, and groom. Our two white steeds were accommodated in a corner of the court, where they reposed after their laborious but glorious campaign, until an opportunity should present itself to secure a new master for them. The poor beasts were so thoroughly worn out that we could not think of offering them for sale until after they should have developed some little flesh between the bone and the skin.

As soon as we were settled in our new abode, we occupied ourselves with inspecting the capital of Tibet and its population. Lhasa is not a large town, its circuit being at the utmost two leagues. It is not surrounded with ramparts, as Chinese towns are; formerly, indeed, it had walls, but these were entirely destroyed in a war made on the Tibetans by the Indians of Bhutan. Around the suburbs, however, are a great number of gardens, the large trees of which form a magnificent wall of verdure for the town. The principal streets of Lhasa are broad, well laid out, and tolerably clean, at least when there is no rain; but the suburbs are revoltingly filthy. The houses, as we have already stated, are in general large, lofty, and handsome; they are built, some of stone, some of brick, and some of mud, but they are all so elaborately covered with lime wash that one cannot distinguish externally any difference in the materials.

In one of the suburban districts, there is a locality where the houses are built of the horns of oxen and sheep; these singular constructions are of extreme solidity and very attractive. The horns of the oxen being smooth and white, and those of the sheep rough and black, these materials are susceptible of infinite combinations, and are arranged accordingly, in all sorts of fantastic designs, the cracks of which are filled up with mortar. These houses are the only buildings that are not lime-washed; the Tibetans have taste enough to leave the materials in their natural aspect, without seeking to improve upon their wild and fantastic beauty. It is easy to conclude that the inhabitants of Lhasa consume an immense quantity of beef and mutton: their horn houses incontestably demonstrate the fact.

The palace of the Grand Lama merits, in every respect, the celebrity which it enjoys throughout the world. North of the town, at the distance of about a mile, there rises a rugged mountain, of slight elevation and of conical form; this, in the midst of the plain, resembles an islet on the bosom of a lake. This mountain is entitled Potala (Mountain of Buddha, or Divine Mountain), and upon it, as upon a great pedestal, the work of nature, the adorers of the Grand Lama have raised the magnificent palace wherein their "Living Divinity" resides in the flesh. This palace is an aggregation of several temples, of various sizes and schemes of decoration. The temple which occupies the center is four stories high and overlooks all the rest; it terminates in a dome, which is entirely covered with plates of gold and surrounded with a peristyle, the columns of which are, in like manner, all covered with gold.

Here the Grand Lama has set up his abode; from the summit of this lofty sanctuary he contemplates, at the great solemnities, his innumerable adorers advancing along the plain and coming to prostrate at the foot of the divine mountain. The secondary palaces, grouped round the great temple, serve as residences for numerous lamas of every order, whose continual occupation it is to serve and do honor to the Living Buddha. Two fine avenues of magnificent trees lead from Lhasa to the Potala, and there one

always finds crowds of foreign pilgrims, telling the beads
of their long Buddhist chaplets, and lamas of the court,
attired in rich costume and mounted on horses splendidly
caparisoned. Around the Potala there is constant motion;
but there is, at the same time, almost uninterrupted silence,
for religious meditations apparently occupy all men's minds.

As soon as we had presented ourselves to the Tibetan
authorities, declaring our characters and the object which
had brought us to Lhasa, we availed ourselves of the semi-
official position we had in this way secured, and got into
communication with the Tibetan and Tartar lamas. Thus,
at last, we were able to begin our work as missioners.

One day, when we were sitting beside our modest hearth,
talking of religious questions with a lama who was well
versed in Buddhist learning, a Chinese dressed in exquisite
style suddenly appeared before us, saying that he was a
merchant and very desirous of buying our goods. We told
him we had nothing to sell.

"How, nothing to sell?"

"Not anything, except indeed these two old saddles."

Then, while he examined our poor merchandise, he addressed to us a thousand questions about our country and
the places we had visited before we came to Lhasa. Shortly
afterwards there arrived a second Chinese; then a third; and
at last two lamas, in costly silk scarves. All these visitors insisted that they wished to buy something from us; they
overwhelmed us with questions, and seemed, at the same
time, to scrutinize with distrust all the corners of our
chamber.

We might say, as often as we liked, that we were not merchants—they insisted they wished to buy. In default of silk,
drapery, or hardware, they would like our saddles; they
turned those around and around in every way, finding them
now perfectly magnificent, now abominal. At last, after
long haggling and cross-questioning, the visitors went off,
promising to return.

The visit of those five individuals occasioned much serious reflection: their manner of acting and speaking was not at all natural. Although they came one after the other, yet they seemed to understand each other perfectly and to aim at the same end by the same means. Their desire to buy something from us was evidently a mere pretext; these people were rather swindlers or spies than real merchants. "Well," we said, "let us wait quietly. Sooner or later we shall see clearly into this affair."

As it was dinner time, we sat down to table; or rather, we remained at the fireside, contemplating the pot, in which a good cut of beef had been boiling for some hours. Samdadchiemba, in his capacity of steward, brought this to the surface of the liquid by means of a large wooden spoon, seized it with his nails, threw it on the end of a board, and cut it into three equal pieces. Then each of us took his portion in his cup, and, with the aid of a few rolls baked in the ashes, tranquilly commenced dinner without troubling ourselves very much about swindlers or spies.

29
The Regent

WE were at our dessert—that is to say, we were about to rinse our cups with some buttered tea—when the two lamas, the pretended merchants, made their reappearance. "The Regent," they said, "awaits you in his palace; he wants to speak to you."

"But," cried we, "does the Regent also, perchance, wish to buy our old saddles?"

"It is not a question about either saddles or merchandise. Rise at once, and follow us to the Regent."

The matter was now beyond a doubt; the Government was desirous of meddling with us—to what end? Was it to do us good or ill? This we could not tell. "Let us go to the Regent," we said, "and trust for the rest to the will of our Heavenly Father."

After having dressed ourselves in our best and put on our majestic caps of foxskin, we said to the senior of our visitors, "We are ready."

"And this young man," he said, pointing to Samdadchiemba, who had turned his eyes upon him with no very affectionate expression.

"This young man is our servant; he will take care of the house in our absence."

"No, no, he must come, too: the Regent wishes to see all three of you."

Samdadchiemba shook his great robe of sheepskin, and

placed, in a very insolent manner, a small black cap over his ear. Then we departed all together after padlocking the door of our lodging.

We went at a rapid pace for about five or six minutes, and then arrived at the palace of the First *Kalon*, the Regent of Tibet. After having crossed a large courtyard, where were assembled a great number of lamas and Chinese, who began to whisper when they saw us appear, we were stopped before a gilded door. Our leader passed through a small corridor on the left, and an instant later the door was opened. At the farther end of an apartment, simply furnished, we perceived a personage sitting with crossed legs on a thick cushion covered with a tiger's skin: this personage was the Regent. With his right hand he made us a sign to approach. We went close up to him, and saluted by placing our caps under our arms. A bench covered with a red carpet stood on our right; on this we were invited to sit down, and we complied immediately.

Meanwhile, the gilded doors were closed, and there remained in the saloon only the Regent and seven individuals, who stood behind him; namely, four lamas of a modest and composed bearing, two Chinese, and a person whom, by his long beard, his turban, and grave countenance, we recognized to be a Mussulman. The Regent was a man of fifty years of age; his large features, mild and remarkably pallid, breathed a truly royal majesty; his dark eyes, shaded by long lashes, were intelligent and gentle. He was dressed in a yellow robe, edged with sable; a ring, adorned with diamonds, hung from his left ear; and his long, jet-black hair was collected together at the top of his head, and fastened by three small gold combs. His large, red cap, set with pearls and surmounted by a coral ball, lay at his side on a green cushion.

When we were seated, the Regent gazed at us for a long while in silence and with very close attention. He turned his head alternately to the right and left, and smiled at us in a half-mocking, half-friendly manner. This sort of pantomime appeared to us so droll, that at last we could not help laughing. "See," we said in French, and in an undertone, "this gentleman seems a good enough fellow; our affair will go on very well."

"Ah," said the Regent, in a very affable tone, "what language is that you speak? I did not understand what you said."

"We spoke the language of our country."

"Well, repeat aloud what you said just now."

"We said, 'This gentleman seems a good-natured enough fellow.' "

The Regent, turning to those who were standing behind him, said, "Do you understand this language?" They all bowed together, and answered that they did not understand it.

"You see, nobody here understands the language of your country. Translate your words into Tibetan."

We said, "In the physiognomy of the First *Kalon* there is expressed much kindliness."

"Ah! you think I have much kindliness; yet I am very ill-natured. Is it not true that I am very ill-natured?" he asked his attendants. They answered merely by smiling.

"You are right," continued the Regent; "I am very kind, for kindness is the duty of a *kalon*. I must be kind towards my people, and also towards strangers." He then addressed to us a long harangue, of which we could comprehend only a few sentences.

When he had finished, we told him that, not being much accustomed to the Tibetan language, we had not fully grasped the sense of his words. The Regent signed to a Chinese, and the latter, stepping forward, translated to us the harangue, of which the following is the outline. We had been summoned without the slightest idea of our being molested: the contradictory reports that had circulated respecting us since our arrival at Lhasa had induced the Regent to question us himself, in order to know where we came from.

"We are from the western sky," we said to the Regent.
"From Calcutta?"
"No; our country is called France."
"You are, doubtless, English?"
"No, we are Frenchmen."
"Can you write?"
"Better than speak."
The Regent, turning around, addressed some words to a lama, who disappeared at once and returned in a moment with paper, ink, and a bamboo point. "Here is paper," said the Regent; "write something."
"In what language—in Tibetan?"
"No; write some letters in your own country's language."
One of us took the paper on his knees, and then wrote this sentence: "What avails it to a man to conquer the whole world, if he lose his own soul?"
"Ah, here are characters of your country! I never saw any like them. And what is the meaning of that?" We wrote the translation in Tibetan, Tartar, and Chinese, and handed it to him.
"I have not been deceived," he said; "you are men of great knowledge. You can write in all languages, and you express thoughts as profound as those we find in the prayer books." He then repeated, slowly moving his head to and fro, "What avails it to a man to conquer the whole world, if he lose his own soul?"
While the Regent and his attendants were indulging in their raptures at our wonderful knowledge, we heard on a sudden, in the courtyard of the palace, the cries of the crowd and the sonorous noise of the Chinese tom-tom. "Here is the Ambassador of Peking," said the Regent. "He wishes to examine you himself. Tell him frankly what concerns you, and rely on my protection: it is I who govern the country." This said, he quitted the saloon with his retinue through a small secret door, and left us alone in this judgment hall.

30

The Chinese Ambassador

T HE idea of falling into the hands of the Chinese made at first a disagreeable impression upon us; and the picture of those horrible persecutions which at different times have afflicted the Christian communities of China seized upon our imagination. But we soon recovered our spirits in the reflection that we were alone, and that, isolated as we were in the midst of Tibet, we could not compromise any one. This thought gave us courage.

"Samdadchiemba," we said to our young neophyte, "now must we show that we are brave men, that we are Christians. This affair will perhaps proceed to great lengths; but let us never lose sight of eternity. If we are treated well, we will thank God for it; if we are maltreated, we will thank Him nevertheless, for we shall have had the happiness of suffering for the Faith. If we are killed, the martyrdom will be a splendid crowning of all our labors. To arrive in heaven after a journey of only eighteen months—would not that be a good journey? would not that be happiness? What do you say, Samdadchiemba?"

"I have never been in fear of death. If I am asked whether I am a Christian, you will see if I tremble."

This excellent frame of mind in Samdadchiemba filled our hearts with joy and completely dissipated the unpleasant impressions which this misadventure had occasioned. We thought for a moment of considering the questions that would probably be put to us and the answers we should give; but we rejected this counsel of mere human prudence, reflecting that the moment had come for us to keep strictly to the injunction which our Saviour addressed to his disciples—that when they were brought before the synagogues, governors, and kings, they should take no thought how or what they should speak. Only, it was agreed that we would salute the mandarin in the French way, and that we would not kneel before him.

After we had waited a few moments, a young Chinese, elegantly dressed and of very graceful manners, came to inform us that Ki-Chan, great Ambassador of the Emperor of China, wished to examine us. We followed our amiable visitor and were ushered into a saloon decorated in the Chinese style. There Ki-Chan was seated upon a sort of throne, about three feet high and covered with red cloth. Before him was a small table of black lacquer, upon which were an inkstand, some pens, some sheets of paper, and a silver vase filled with snuff. Below the throne were four scribes, two on the right and two on the left. The remainder of the saloon was occupied by a great number of Chinese and Tibetans, who had put on their holiday dress to attend the inquiry.

Ki-Chan, although sixty years old, seemed to us full of strength and vigor. His face was, without contradiction, the most noble, elegant and intellectual we had seen amongst the Chinese. We took off our caps to him, and made him one of our best bows. " 'Tis well, 'tis well," he said; "follow your own customs. I have been told you speak correctly the language of Peking. I want to talk with you for a moment."

"We make many blunders in speaking, but your marvelous understanding will be able to remedy the obscurity of our words."

"Why, that is pure Pekingese. You Frenchmen possess a great facility for all learning. You are Frenchmen, are you not?"

"Yes, we are Frenchmen."

"Oh, I know the French. There were formerly a great many of them at Peking; I used to see some of them."

"You must have know them, too, at Canton, when you were imperial commissioner?"

This reminiscence furrowed the forehead of our judge; he took an abundant pinch of snuff out of his box, and threw it up his nose in very bad humor. "Yes, that is true: I have seen many Europeans at Canton. You are of the religion of the Lord of Heaven, are you not?"

"Certainly we are; moreover, preachers of that religion."

"I know, I know. You have come hither, doubtless, to preach that religion?"

"We have no other object."

"Have you traveled through many other countries?"

"We have traveled over all China and Tartary, and now we are in the capital of Tibet."

"With whom did you live when you were in China?"

"We do not answer questions of that sort."

"And if I command you to do so?"

"We would not obey."

Here the irritated judge struck the table with his fist.

"You know," we said, "that Christians have no fear. Why seek, then, to intimidate us?"

"Where did you learn Chinese?"

"In China."

"In what place?"

"A little everywhere."

"And the Tartar you know—where did you learn it?"

"In Mongolia, in the Land of Grass."

After some trifling questions, Ki-Chan told us that we must be tired, and invited us to seat ourselves. Then, suddenly changing his tone and manner, he addressed Samdad-chiemba, who had been standing a little behind us. "And you," he said, in a dry and angry voice, "whence are you?"

"I am from Chi-Tu-Ssu."

"What is Chi-Tu-Ssu? Is there anyone who knows it?"

"Chi-Tu-Ssu is in Sab-chuan."

"Ah, you are from Sab-chuan, in the Province of Kansu. Son of the Central Nation, on your knees!" Samdadchiemba turned pale. "On your knees!" repeated the Ambassador in a thundering voice.

Samdadchiemba fell on his knees, saying, "On my knees, standing, or sitting, 'tis all the same to me: a man of labor and fatigue, such as I am, is not accustomed to take his ease."

"Ah, you are from Kansu," said the judge, taking large pinches of snuff. "Ah, you are from Kansu; you are a child of the Central Nation! Very well; in that case, it is within my province to deal with you. Son of the Central Nation, answer me and see that you don't scatter lies. Where did you meet these two foreigners? How did you become attached to their service?"

Samdadchiemba gave, with perfect self-confidence, a long history of his life, which seemed to interest the audience. Then he related how he had made our acquaintance in Tartary, and the reasons that had induced him to follow us. Our young neophyte spoke with dignity and, moreover, with a prudence which we had not expected.

"Why did you adopt the religion of the Lord of Heaven? Don't you know that this is forbidden by the great Emperor?"

"This most lowly one adopted that religion because it is the only true religion. How could I believe that the great Emperor proscribed a religion which orders man to do good and to avoid evil?"

"That is true: the religion of the Lord of Heaven is holy; I know it. Why did you enter the service of these foreigners? Don't you know that the law forbids that?"

"How should an ignorant man, such as I am, know who is a foreigner, and who not? These men always showed me kindness, always exhorted me to practice virtue. Why should I not follow them?"

"How much wages do they pay you?"

"I accompany them to save my soul, not to get money. My masters have never let me want for rice and clothes, and with that I am satisfied."

"Are you married?"

"As I was a lama before adopting the religion of the Lord of Heaven, I have never been married."

The judge then laughingly addressed an indelicate question to Samdadchiemba, who lowered his eyes and remained silent. One of us, rising, said to Ki-Chan: "Our religion not only prohibits the commission of impure actions, but also the thinking or speaking of them. We are even forbidden to listen to indecent expressions."

These words, pronounced with calmness and solemnity, raised a slight blush on the face of His Excellency, the Ambassador of China. "I know," he said, "I know the religion of the Lord of Heaven is holy. I know it, for I have read its books of doctrine: he who would strictly keep all its precepts would be a man without reproach." He made a sign to Samdadchiemba to rise. Then, turning to us, he said: "It is night. You must be tired. It is time to take supper; you may go. Tomorrow if I want you, I will send for you."

31
Regent's Hospitality

AMBASSADOR Ki-Chan was quite right: it was very late, and the various emotions which had been furnished to us in the course of the evening had not by any means supplied the place of supper. On leaving the Chinese-Tibetan pretorium, we were accosted by a venerable lama, who informed us that the Regent awaited us. We crossed the court, which was illuminated by some red lanterns; turned to the right and ascended a perilous staircase, prudently holding to our conductor's robe; then, after traversing a long terrace, in the dubious light of the stars, we were brought into the presence of the Regent. The large and lofty room was splendidly lighted by butter-oil lamps; the walls, the ceiling, even the floor, were all covered with gilding and brilliant colors. The Regent was alone. He bade us sit down near himself on a rich carpet, and endeavored to express by his words, and still more by his gestures, how deep an interest he felt in us. Above all, we clearly grasped that he was making arrangements to keep us from starving.

Our pantomime was interrupted by the arrival of a person who, upon entering, left his slippers at the door. This was the governor of the Kashmir Mussulmans, of whom a large colony dwelt permanently in Lhasa. After having saluted the company, by raising his hand to his forehead and pronouncing the formula *"Salaamalek!"* he leaned against a column in the center of the room. The Mussul-

man governor spoke Chinese very well, and the Regent had
accordingly sent for him to act as interpreter. Immediately
upon his arrival, a servant placed before us a small table, and
supper was served to us at the expense of the Tibetan Government. All of a sudden we missed Samdadchiemba; we
asked what had become of him. "He is with my servants,"
answered the Regent. "Do not trouble yourselves on his
account; he wants for nothing."

During and after the repast, there was much inquiry
about France and the countries we had visited. Then the
Regent, pointing to the pictures that adorned his room,
asked whether we could ourselves paint any such. "We
cannot paint," was our answer; "study, and the preaching
of the doctrine of the Lord of Heaven, are our only occupations."

"Oh, don't tell me you cannot paint. I know that the
people of your country are very skillful in that art."

"Yes, those are who make it their employment; but we
clergymen are not in the habit of exercising it."

"Though you may not practice this art especially, yet you
are not quite unacquainted with it. Doubtless you can draw
geographical maps?"

"No, we cannot."

"What! On your journey did you never sketch, did you
never make a map?"

"Never."

"Oh, that is impossible!"

The pertinacity of the Regent in questioning us on this
subject made us pause to reflect; presently we expressed
the surprise we felt at all these inquiries. "I see," he answered, "that you are straight-forward, honest men. I will
speak frankly to you. The Chinese are very suspicious. You
are aware of that; you have been long enough in China to
know it as well as I do. Well, the Chinese believe that you
are traveling through foreign kingdoms to explore and to
draw maps of them. If you do draw, if you make geographi-

cal maps, admit it without fear; rely on my protection."

Evidently the Regent was afraid of an invasion; he fancied, perhaps, that we were charged with planning the route for some formidable army ready to overwhelm Tibet. We endeavored to dissipate his fears, and to assure him of the extremely peaceful views of the French Government. We admitted, however, that amongst our effects there were a great number of drawings and geographical maps, and that we had even a map of Tibet. At these words, the face of the Regent was suddenly contracted; and we hastened to add, in order to quiet him, that all our drawings and maps were printed, and that we were not their authors. We took the opportunity to tell the Regent and the Kashmir governor of the geographical knowledge of the Europeans. They were greatly astonished when we said that, with us, children of ten and twelve years old possessed a good idea of all the kingdoms of the world.

The conversation extended far into the night. At last the Regent rose and asked us whether we did not feel in want of a little repose. "We only waited," we answered, "for the permission of the *Kalon* to return to our lodgings."

"Your lodgings? I have ordered that an apartment be prepared for you in my palace. You will sleep here tonight: tomorrow you can return to your house."

We sought to excuse ourselves from accepting the kind offer of the Regent, but soon became aware that we were not at liberty to refuse what we had been simple enough to consider a compliment. We were regular prisoners. We took leave of the Regent rather coolly, and followed an individual who, after crossing a great many rooms and corridors, ushered us into a sort of closet. This we might fairly call a prison, as we were not to be permitted to leave it for any other place. There had been prepared for us two couches, which, no doubt, were infinitely superior to our own beds; nevertheless, we regretted our poor pallets, whereon we had so long enjoyed a free and independent sleep throughout our travels in the desert.

Lamas and attendants of the Regent came immediately in great numbers to see us. Those who had gone to bed got up, and soon we heard, in this vast palace, lately so calm and silent, doors open and shut, and the rapid steps of the curious sounding in the passage. Crowds thronged around us and examined us with insupportable avidity. In all those eyes staring at us there was neither sympathy nor ill will; there was simply vapid curiosity. To all these individuals around us, we represented merely a kind of zoological phenomenon. Oh, how hard it is to be exposed thus to an indifferent multitude! When we thought that these troublesome people had sufficiently stared and whispered, and ought to be satisfied, we informed them that we were going to bed, and that we should feel extremely obliged if they would be kind enough to retire.

Every one bowed; some of them even were polite enough to put out their tongues at us; but nobody stirred. It was evident that they wished to discover how we should behave on going to bed. This desire seemed to us somewhat misplaced; but we thought we would submit to it up to a certain point. Accordingly we knelt down, made the sign of the cross, and recited aloud our evening prayer. As soon as we commenced, the whispering ceased, and a religious silence prevailed. When the prayer was finished, we once more invited the crowd to leave us—and, in order to add efficacy to our words, we extinguished the light. The crowd, thus plunged into deep darkness, laughed heartily, and retired gropingly. We closed the door of our prison and lay down to rest.

When we stretched on the beds provided by the First *Kalon*, we felt much more disposed to talk than to sleep. We experienced a certain pleasure in rehearsing the adventures of the day. The pretended merchants who wanted to purchase our saddles, our appearance before the Regent, the examination we had undergone by Ambassador Ki-Chan, our supper at the expense of the public treasury, our long conversation with the Regent—all appeared to us a phantasmagoria. It seemed as though our whole day had been a long nightmare. Our journey itself, our arrival at Lhasa, everything seemed incredible. We asked one another whether it was true that we Catholic missioners were really in the state of the Grand Lama, in the capital of Tibet, sleeping in the very palace of the Regent. All these events, past and present, clashed in our heads.

The future, especially, appeared to us enveloped in thick, dark clouds. How was all this to end? Would they say to us, "You are free; go wherever you please"? Would they keep us in this prison? Or would they strangle us? These reflections were well calculated to chill the heart and to cause a headache. But trust in God is a grand thing in such trials! How happy is one in feeling oneself supported by Providence, when one is thus left alone, abandoned, and destitute of succor. "Oh," said we to each other, "let us be prepared for the worst, relying upon the protection of our Heavenly Father! Not a single hair will fall from our heads without His permission."

We went to sleep amid these considerations, but our slumber was light and disturbed. As soon as dawn appeared, the door of our cell was gently opened, and the Mussulman governor entered. He took a seat at our side, between the two couches, and asked us in kind, affectionate tones whether we had spent a good night. He then presented us with a basket of cakes, made by his family, and some dried fruits from Ladak; and we were deeply touched by this attention, which seemed to announce that we had met with a sincere and devoted friend. The governor was thirty-two years old. His face, full of nobleness and majesty, revealed at the same time a kindness and candor well calculated to arouse our confidence. His looks, his words, his deportment, everything about him, seemed to express that he felt

a very lively interest in us. He had come especially to acquaint us with what would be done during the day, with
reference to us.

"In the morning," he said, "the Tibetan authorities will
go with you to your lodgings. They will put a seal upon all
your effects. These will then be taken before the tribunal,
and be examined by the Regent and the Chinese Ambassador, in your presence. If you have no manuscript maps in
your baggage, you need fear nothing; you will not be
molested in any way. If, on the contrary, you have any such
maps, you would do well to let me know beforehand, as in
this case we may perhaps find some way to arrange the
affair. I am very intimate with the Regent [this we had,
indeed, observed the night before during our supper], and
it is he himself who directed me to make to you this con-
fidential communication." He then added, in an undertone,
that all these difficulties were instigated against us by
the Chinese, against the will of the Tibetan Government.

We answered the governor that we had not a single
manuscript map; and we then gave him, in detail, a statement of all the articles that were in our trunks. "Since they
are to be examined today, you will be able to judge for
yourself whether we are people to be believed."

The countenance of the Mussulman brightened. "Your
words," he said, "quite reassure me. None of the articles
you have described can at all compromise you. Maps are
feared in this country—extremely feared, indeed; especially
since the affair of a certain Englishman named Moorcroft,
who introduced himself into Lhasa under the pretense of
being a Kashmirian. After a sojourn there of twelve years,
he departed; but he was murdered on his way to Ladak.
Amongst his effects was found a numerous collection of
maps and plans, which he had drawn during his stay at
Lhasa. This circumstance has made the Chinese authorities
very suspicious on this subject. As you do not draw maps,

you are all right. I will go now and tell the Regent what I have heard from you."

When the governor had left us, we rose, for we had remained in bed without ceremony during his long visit. After having offered up our morning prayer and disposed our hearts to patience and resignation, we ate the breakfast which had been sent to us by order of the Regent. It consisted of a plate of rolls stuffed with sugar and minced meat, and a pot of richly buttered tea. But we gave the preference to the cakes and dried fruit which the governor had presented to us.

32

The Examination

THREE lama ushers soon came and announced to us the order of the day; namely, that our luggage was to be inspected. We submitted respectfully to the orders of the Tibetan authority, and proceeded to our lodgings, accompanied by a numerous escort all the way. From the palace of the Regent to our habitation, we observed great excitement: people were sweeping the streets, removing the dirt, and decorating the front of the houses with large strips of paper, yellow and red. We asked ourselves what all this meant, for whom were all these demonstrations of honor and respect. Suddenly we heard behind us loud acclamations. Turning around, we saw the Regent advancing, mounted on a magnificent white charger and surrounded by numerous horsemen. We arrived at our lodgings at about the same time he did. We opened the padlock by which the door was fastened, and requested the Regent to honor us by entering our apartments.

Samdadchiemba, whom we had not seen since our audience with the Chinese Ambassador, was there, too. He was quite stupefied, for he could not comprehend these proceedings. The servants of the Regent, with whom he had passed the night, could not give him any information. We said to him some words of encouragement, giving him to understand that we were not yet quite on the eve of martyrdom.

The Regent took a seat in the middle of our room, on

a gilded chair which had been brought from the palace for this purpose, and asked whether what he saw in our room was all we possessed.

"Yes; that is all we possess; neither more nor less. These are all our resources for invading Tibet."

"There is satire in your words," said the Regent. "I have never fancied you such dangerous people. What is that?" he added, pointing to a crucifix we had hung on the wall.

"Ah, if you really knew what that is, you would not say that we are not formidable! For by that we plan to conquer China, Tartary, and Tibet." The Regent laughed, for he saw only a joke in our words, which yet were so real and serious.

A scribe sat down at the feet of the Regent, and made an inventory of our trunks, clothes, and kitchen implements. A lighted lamp was brought, and the Regent took from a small purse which hung from his neck a golden seal, which was applied to all our baggage. Nothing was omitted: our old boots, the very pins of our traveling tent, were all daubed with red wax and solemnly marked with the seal of the Grand Lama.

When this long ceremony was completed, the Regent informed us that we must now proceed to the tribunal. Some porters were sent for, and found in very brief time; a lama of the police had only to present himself in the street and summon, in the name of the law, all the pass-ers-by—men, women, and children—to come into the house immediately and assist the Government. At Lhasa the system of enforced labor is in a most prosperous and flourishing state, the Tibetans accepting it with entire willingness and good grace.

When enough laborers were gathered, all our goods were distributed among them until the room was completely cleared; then the procession to the tribunal set out with great pomp. A Tibetan cavalryman, his drawn sword in hand and a light musket at his side, led the parade; after

him came the troop of porters, marching between two lines
of lama satellites; the Regent, on his white charger, surrounded by a mounted guard of honor, followed our baggage; and last, behind the Regent, marched the two poor
Catholic missioners, who had, by way of suite, a not-very-
agreeable crowd of gapers. Our mien was not particularly
imposing: led like malefactors, or at least like suspected
persons, we could only lower our eyes and modestly pass
through the large crowd that thronged our way. Such a
position was, indeed, very painful and humiliating; but the
remembrance of our holy Saviour, dragged through the
streets of Jerusalem, was sufficient to mitigate the bitterness
with which we were afflicted. We prayed to Him to sanctify
our humiliations by His own, and to accept them in remembrance of His passion.

When we arrived at the tribunal, the Chinese Ambassador attended by his staff was already in his place. The Regent addressed him: "You wish to examine the effects of
these strangers. Here they are; examine them. These men
are neither rich, nor powerful, as you suppose." There was
vexation in the tone of the Regent, and, at bottom, he was
naturally enough annoyed at this part of policeman which
he had to play.

Ki-Chan asked us if we had no more than two trunks.
"Only two; everything has been brought here. There remains in our house not a rag, not a bit of paper."

"What have you got in your two trunks?"

"Here are the keys. Open the trunks, empty them, and
examine them at your pleasure."

Ki-Chan blushed and moved back; his Chinese delicacy
was offended. "Do these trunks belong to me?" he asked
with emotion. "Have I the right to open them? If anything
should be missed afterwards, what would you say?"

"You need not be afraid; our religion forbids us to judge
our neighbor rashly."

"Open your trunks yourselves. I want to know what they

contain; it is my duty to do so; but you alone have the right to touch what belongs to you."

We broke the seal of the Grand Lama, the padlock was removed and these two trunks, which had been the target of all eyes for a long time past, were at last opened to the general gaze. We took out the contents, one article after another, and displayed them on a large table. First came some French and Latin volumes, then some Chinese and Tartar books, then church linens, ornaments, sacred vessels, rosaries, crosses, medals, and a magnificent collection of lithographs.

All the spectators were absorbed in contemplation of this small European museum. They opened their eyes wide, nudged each other with their elbows, and smacked their tongues in token of admiration. None of them had ever seen anything so beautiful, so rich, so marvelous. Everything yellow they considered gold. The faces of all brightened, and they seemed entirely to forget that we were suspected of being dangerous people. The Tibetans politely put out their tongues and scratched their ears at us; and the Chinese made us the most obsequious bows. Our bag of medals, especially, attracted attention, and it seemed to be expected that, before we left the court, we should make a large distribution of these dazzling gold pieces.

The Regent and Ki-Chan, whose minds were elevated above those of the vulgar, and who certainly did not covet our treasure, nevertheless forgot their character as judges. The sight of our beautiful colored pictures transported them quite out of themselves. The Regent kept his hands joined, and preserved a continuous stare with his mouth open, whilst Ki-Chan, showing off his knowledge, explained how the French were the most distinguished artists in the world. At one time, he said, he knew at Peking a French missioner, who painted portraits which resembled the persons so much that they frightened you. The missioner "kept his paper concealed in the sleeve of his robe, took the likeness as it were by stealth, and, in a whiff, all was done."

Ki-Chan asked us if we had watches, telescopes, magic lanterns, and so forth. We thereupon opened a small box which no one had hitherto noticed, and which contained a microscope. We adjusted its various parts, and no one in our audience had eyes but for this singular machine, which they took to be pure gold, and which, certainly, was about to perform wondrous things. Ki-Chan alone knew what a microscope was. He gave an explanation of it to the audience, with great pretension and vanity. He then asked us to put some animalcula on the glass.

We looked at His Excellency out of the corner of the eye, and then took the microscope to pieces, joint by joint, and put it in the box. "We thought," said we to Ki-Chan, with a formal air, "that we came here to undergo judgment, and not to play a comedy."

"What judgment?" exclaimed he, abruptly. "We wished to examine your effects, ascertain who you really are, and that is all."

"And the maps; you do not mention them."

"Oh, yes—yes! That is the great point. Where are your maps?"

"Here they are." And we displayed the three maps we had: a map of the world, the two hemispheres upon the projection of Mercator, and a Chinese Empire.

The appearance of these maps seemed a thunderclap to the Regent. The poor man changed color three or four times in the course of a minute, as if we had shown him his death warrant. "It is fortunate for us," said we to Ki-Chan, "that we have met with you in this country. If, by ill luck, you had not been here, we should have been utterly unable to convince the Tibetan authorities that these maps are not our own drawing. But an instructed man like yourself, conversant with European matters, will at once see that these maps are not our own work."

Ki-Chan was evidently much flattered by the compliment. "Oh, it is evident," said he, at the first glance, "that these maps are printed." "Look here," said he to the Regent;

"these maps were not drawn by these men; they were printed in France. You cannot distinguish that, but I have long been used to objects which are the productions of the western heaven."

At these words the face of the Regent became radiant. He looked at us with a look of satisfaction, and made a gracious movement of the head, as much as to say, "It is well; you are honest people."

We could not get off without giving a little geographical lecture. We yielded, as a matter of kindness, to the wishes of the Regent and the Chinese Ambassador and pointed out, on the Mercator map, the countries of China, Tartary, and Tibet, and all the other countries of the globe. The Regent was amazed at seeing how far we were from our native land, and what a long journey we had been obliged to make, by land and water, to pay him a visit in the capital of Tibet. He regarded us with astonishment, and then raised the thumb of his right hand, saying, "You are men like that!" In the figurative language of the Tibetans, this signified, "You are men of a superlative stamp!"

After recognizing the principal points of Tibet, the Regent inquired the location of Calcutta. "Here," we said, pointing to a little round speck on the borders of the sea.

"And Lhasa—where then is Lhasa?"

"Here it is."

The eyes and fingers of the Regent went from Lhasa to Calcutta, and from Calcutta to Lhasa. "The Pelings of Calcutta are very near our frontiers," said he, making a grimace, and shaking his head. "But no matter," he added; "here are the Himalaya Mountains."

The lecture in geography being ended, the maps were folded up and placed in their respective cases, and we passed on to religious subjects. Ki-Chan had long since become acquainted with these matters. When he was viceroy of the Province of Pechili, he had persecuted the Christians so much that he had had numerous opportunities to

make himself familiar with everything connected with
Catholic worship; and he now displayed his knowledge. He
explained the images, the sacred vessels, the ornaments. He
even informed the company that in the box of holy oils
there was a famous remedy for people at death's door. During all these explanations, the Regent was thoughtful and
abstracted; his eyes constantly turned towards a large imple-
ment for making hosts. These long iron pincers, terminating in two large lips, seemed to act powerfully on his imagination. He gave us an inquiring look, as if to ask if this
frightful machine were not something like an instrument
of torture. He was only reassured upon viewing some wafers
that we kept in a box, for he then comprehended the use
of this strange object.

The worthy Regent was joyous and triumphant when he
saw that we had nothing in our possession calculated to
compromise us. "Well," said he to the Chinese Ambassador,
with a sneer, "what do you think of these men? What must
we do with them? These men are Frenchmen, they are
ministers of the religion of the Lord of Heaven, they are
honest men; we must leave them in peace."

These flattering words were received in the saloon with
a murmur of approbation, and the two missioners said,
from the bottom of their hearts, *"Deo gratias!"*

The porters shouldered our luggage, and we returned to
our lodging with undoubtedly greater alacrity and lighter
hearts than we had had when we left it. The news of our
vindication soon spread through the town, and the Tibetan
people hastened from all quarters to congratulate us. They
saluted us heartily. When we had refurnished our apartments, we gave a small reward to the porters, in order that
they might drink our health in a pot of Tibetan small beer
and appreciate the magnanimity of the French, who do
not make people work for nothing.

33

Friends in Lhasa

WHEN everyone had gone away, we resumed our accustomed solitude, and, as solitude induces reflection, we discovered two important things: in the first place, we had not yet dined; and in the second, our horses were no longer in the stable. Whilst we were considering how to get something quickly cooked and how to find our horses, we saw at the threshold of our door the Mussulman governor. This excellent man relieved us from our double embarrassment. Having realized that our attendance at the court of inquiry would not allow us time to make our pot boil, he came, followed by two servants carrying a basket of provisions, with a repast he had prepared for us.

"And our horses—can you give us any information about them?" we asked him. "We no longer see them in the court."

"I was going to tell you about them. Since yesterday evening, they have been in the Regent's stables. During your absence they have felt neither hunger nor thirst. I heard you say you intended to sell them—is that so?"

"Oh, quite so. These animals ruin us; and yet they are so thin, no one will buy them."

"The Regent wants to buy them."

"The Regent!"

"Yes, the Regent himself. Do not smile; it is no jest. How much do you want for them?"

"Oh, whatever he likes to give."

"Well, then, your horses are purchased!" And so saying, the Kashmirian unrolled a small packet he had under his arm, and laid upon the table two silver ingots, weighing ten ounces each. "Here," said he, "is the price of your two horses."

We thought our beasts, worn and attenuated as they were, not worth the money, and we conscientiously said so to the governor; but it was impossible to alter the transaction, which had been all settled beforehand. The Regent made out that our horses, although thin, were of an excellent breed, since they had not succumbed beneath the fatigues of our long journey. Besides, they had in his eyes a special value, because they had passed through many countries, and particularly because they had fed on the pastures of Kumbum, the native place of Tsong-Kaba.

Twenty extra ounces of silver in our low purse was almost a fortune. We could be generous with it; so, on the spot, we took one of the ingots and placed it on Samdadchiemba's knees. "This is for you," we said; "you will be able with it to clothe yourself in holiday dress from head to foot."

Samdadchiemba thanked us coldly and awkwardly; then the muscles of his face relaxed, his nostrils dilated, and his large mouth broke into a smile. At last he could not restrain his joy; he rose and made his ingot leap in the air twice or thrice, crying, "This is a famous day!" And Samdadchiemba was right. This day, so sadly begun, had been fortunate beyond anything we could have expected. We had now, at Lhasa, an honorable position, and we were to be allowed to labor freely in the propagation of the Gospel.

The next day was still more lucky for us than its predecessor, putting, as it were, a climax to our prosperity. In the morning we proceeded, accompanied by the Kashmirian governor, to the palace of the Regent, to whom we desired to express our gratitude for the manifestations of interest

with which he had honored us. We were received with
kindness and cordiality. He told us, in confidence, that the
Chinese were jealous of our being at Lhasa; but that we
might count on his protection, and reside freely in the
country, without any one having a right to interfere
with us.

"You are very badly lodged," added he. "Your room
seemed to me dirty, small, and uncomfortable. I would have
strangers like you, men come from so great a distance, well
treated at Lhasa. In your country of France, do you not
treat strangers well?"

"We treat them excellently. Oh, if you could but go there
some day, you would see how our Emperor would receive
you!"

"Strangers are guests. You must leave your present abode;
I have ordered a suitable lodging to be prepared for you
in one of my houses."

We accepted this generous offer with grateful thanks. To
be lodged comfortably and free of expense was not a thing
for men in our position to despise; but we appreciated,
above all, the advantage of residing in one of the Regent's
own houses. So signal a favor, such emphatic protection on
the part of the Tibetan authorities, could not but give us
great moral influence with the inhabitants of Lhasa and
facilitate our apostolic mission. On leaving the palace, we
proceeded, without loss of time, to visit the house which
had been assigned to us. It was superb—charming! The
same evening we effected our removal, and took possession
of our new dwelling.

Our first care was to erect in our house a small chapel.
We selected the largest and best apartment; we papered it
as neatly as possible; and we then adorned it with holy
images. Oh! how our hearts overflowed with joy when we
were at length allowed to pray publicly at the foot of the
cross, in the very heart of the capital of Buddhism, which
probably had never before beheld the sign of our redemp-

tion. What a comfort to us to be able, at length, to announce the words of life to the ears of these poor people, sitting for so many ages in the shadow of death! This little chapel was certainly poor, but it was to our minds that hundredfold which God has promised to those who renounce all things for His service. Our hearts were so full that we thought the happiness we then enjoyed was indeed cheaply bought by our two years of suffering and tribulation in the desert.

Every one at Lhasa wanted to visit the chapel of the Catholic lamas. Many, after satisfying themselves with asking a few explanations as to the meaning of the images they beheld, went away, putting off till some other time further instruction in the holy doctrine of the Lord of Heaven; but several felt deeply impressed and seemed to attach great importance to the study of the truths we had come to announce. Every day thereafter they came to us; they read with attention the summary of the Christian religion, which we had composed at the lamasery of Kumbum, and entreated us to teach them the "true prayers."

The Tibetans were not the only persons who seemed zealous to study our holy religion. Among the Chinese, the secretaries of Ambassador Ki-Chan often came to visit us, to hear about the great doctrine of the west. One of them, to whom we had lent some Christian works written in Tartar-Manchu, was convinced of the truth of Christianity and of the necessity of embracing it, but he had not courage enough to make an open confession of faith whilst he was attached to the embassy; he wished to wait until he should be free to return to his country. God grant that his good intention may not vanish!

A physician, a native of the Province of Yunnan, displayed more courage. This young man, since his arrival at Lhasa, had led so strange a life that every one called him "the Chinese hermit." He never went out except to visit his patients, and ordinarily he visited only the poor. In vain the wealthy solicited his attendance; he disdained to notice their invitations unless compelled by necessity to obtain aid, for he never took anything from the poor, to whose service he had devoted himself. The time not absorbed in visiting his patients, he consecrated to study; indeed, he spent the greater part of the night over his books. He slept little, and took throughout the day only one single meal of barley mush, never eating meat. One needed, indeed, only to see him to be convinced that he led a hard and self-denying life: his face was extremely pale and thin, and, although he was not more than thirty years old, his hair was almost entirely white.

One day he paid us a visit while we were reading our Breviary in our little chapel. He stopped short a few steps from the door, and waited in grave silence. A large colored picture, representing the Crucifixion, had no doubt attracted his attention; for, as soon as we had finished our prayers, he asked us abruptly, and without stopping to make the usual salutations, to explain to him the meaning of the Crucifixion. He remained standing with arms crossed and gazing intently on the picture of the Crucifixion for half an hour; at length his eyes were filled with tears, he extended his arms toward the Christ, fell on his knees, struck the earth thrice with his forehead, and rose, exclaiming, "That is the only Buddha that men ought to worship!" He then turned to us and, after making a profound bow, said: "You are my masters. Accept me as your disciple."

All this surprised us greatly. We could not help believing that a powerful impulse of grace had moved his heart. We briefly explained to him the principle points of the Christian religion. To all we told him, he simply replied with an expression of faith truly astonishing, "I believe!" We presented him with a small crucifix of gilt copper, and asked him if he would accept it. His answer was an earnest inclination of the head; he then requested us to give him a cord, and he immediately hung the cross round his neck.

That done, he asked what prayer he ought to recite before the cross.

"We will lend you," we said, "some Chinese books, wherein you will find explanations of the doctrine, and numerous forms of prayer."

"My masters, that is well; but I wish to have a short and easy prayer, which I can learn immediately, and repeat often and everywhere."

We taught him to say, "Jesus, Saviour of the world, have mercy on me." For fear of forgetting these words, he wrote them on a piece of paper, which he placed in a small purse, suspended from his girdle. He then went away, assuring us that the recollection of this day would never be effaced from his memory.

This young physician applied himself with ardor to learn the truths of the Christian religion; but the most remarkable circumstance was that he took no pains to hide the faith he had in his heart. When he came to visit us, or when we met him in the streets, he always had the crucifix glittering on his breast; and he never failed to approach us with the words, "Jesus, Saviour of the world, have mercy on me." It was the form of salutation which he had adopted.

34

Our Friend the Regent

WHILST we were making efforts to spread the Gospel amongst the population of Lhasa, we did not neglect the endeavor to sow the divine seed also in the very palace of the Regent, and this not without the hope of reaping there one day a precious harvest. Since our quasi-trial, our intercourse with the Regent had become frequent and even intimate. Almost every evening, when he had finished his labors of state, he invited us to partake with him of his Tibetan repast, to which he always added for us some dishes cooked in the Chinese fashion. Our conversations generally extended far into the night.

The Regent was a man of extraordinary ability. Of humble origin, he had within three years raised himself, by his own merits, to the dignity of First *Kalon*. Before reaching that eminence, he had always fulfilled arduous and laborious functions; he had frequently traversed, in all directions, the immense regions of Tibet, either to make war, or to negotiate with the neighboring states, or to inspect the conduct of the governors of the various provinces. So active and busy a life was apparently incompatible with study, but it had not prevented him from acquiring a profound knowledge of Lamaistic works. Every one concurred in saying that the knowledge of the most renowned lamas was inferior to that of the Regent.

The facility with which he conducted public business also

was a matter of especial admiration. One day we were with him when they brought him a great many rolls of paper, dispatches from the provinces. A secretary unrolled them, one after the other, and, bending on one knee, gave them to him to read. The Regent hastily ran his eye over them, without interrupting the conversation with us. As soon as he had grasped the contents of a dispatch, he took his bamboo style and wrote his orders at the bottom of the roll, and thus transacted all his affairs with promptitude and as if in sport. We are not competent to judge of the literary merit that was attributed to the First *Kalon*; but we can say that we never saw Tibetan writing so beautiful as his.

The Regent was very fond of engaging in religious discussions, and they most frequently formed the subject of our conversations. At the very beginning he spoke to us these remarkable words: "All your long journey you have undertaken solely with a religious object. You are quite right, for religion is the thing most essential to man. I see that the French and the Tibetans have the same view on that subject; we do not resemble the Chinese, who hold the soul of no account. Yet your religion is not the same as ours. It is important we should ascertain which is the true one. Let us, then, examine both carefully and sincerely. If yours is right, we will adopt it. How could we refuse to do so? If, on the contrary, ours is the true religion, I believe you will have the good sense to follow it."

These dispositions seemed to us excellent; we could not at that stage desire better. We began the study with Christianity, for the Regent, always amiable and polished with us, said that, as we were his guests, our belief ought to have the honor of priority. To our great astonishment, he did not seem surprised at anything we said.

"Your religion," the Regent repeatedly told us, "is conformable with ours; the truths are the same. We differ only in the explanations. Of what you have seen and heard in Tartary and Tibet, there is, doubtless, much that is blameworthy; but you must not forget that the numerous errors and superstitions you may have observed were introduced by ignorant lamas, and that they are rejected by well-informed Buddhists." He admitted, between his religion and ours, only two points of difference: the origin of the world, and the transmigration of souls. But actually the belief of the Regent, though it here and there seemed to approximate Catholic doctrine, resulted in a vast pantheism. He claimed that we also arrived at the same result, and he did his best to convince us of this.

The Tibetan language, essentially religious and mystic, conveys with much clearness and precision all the ideas respecting the human soul and divinity. Unfortunately, we were not sufficiently versed in this language, and were compelled, in our conversations with the Regent, to have recourse to the Kashmirian governor to interpret for us; but, as he himself was not very skillful in rendering metaphysical ideas into Chinese, it was often difficult to understand each other.

One day the Regent said to us: "The truth is clear in itself, but if you envelope it in obscure words, one cannot perceive it. So long as we are obliged to communicate in Chinese, it will be impossible to make ourselves intelligible to each other. We shall never be able to discuss the matter to advantage, till you can speak the Tibetan language fluently."

We quite concurred in the justice of this observation. We replied to the Regent that the study of the Tibetan tongue was a great object of solicitude with us, and that we labored hard at it every day. "If you like," said he, "I will facilitate your acquisition of it." Thereupon he called a servant and said a few words to him. After the servant had departed, a youth, elegantly dressed, came in and saluted us with much grace.

"This is my nephew," said the Regent. "I present him to you as both tutor and pupil. He will spend the whole day with you, and you will thus have the opportunity of practicing the Tibetan language; in return, you will give him lessons in Chinese and Manchu." We gratefully adopted this proposition, and were enabled by this means to make rapid progress in the language of the country.

The Regent was very fond of talking about France. During our long visits he asked us a number of questions about the manners, customs, and productions of our country. All we told him of the steamboats, the railways, the balloons, gas lights, telegraph, daguereotype, and all our industrial products, completely amazed him and gave him an immense idea of the grandeur and power of France. One day when we were talking to him of observatories and astronomical instruments, he asked if we would allow him to examine closely the curious machine which we kept in a box; he meant the microscope. As we were in a better humor and infinitely more amiable than when the officers inspected our property, we readily agreed to satisfy the curiosity of the Regent.

One of us ran to our residence, and returned immediately with the wonderful instrument. While adjusting it, we tried to give our audience some notion of the science of optics. But we saw that the theory did not excite much enthusiasm, and so we proceeded at once to the practice. We asked if one of the company would be so good as to procure us a louse. The article was easier to find than a butterfly. A noble lama, secretary to His Excellency, the First *Kalon*, had merely to put his hand under his silk dress at his armpit, and an extremely vigorous louse was at our disposition. We seized it by the sides with our nippers, but the lama forthwith opposed this proceeding and insisted upon putting a stop to the experiment, on the ground that we were to cause the death of a living being.

"Do not be afraid," we said; "your louse is only taken by the skin. Besides, he seems strong enough to get over the pressure, even were it greater."

The Regent, who, as we have before mentioned, had religious theories superior to those of the common herd, told the lama to be silent and to allow us to proceed. We continued the experiment and fixed in the glass the poor little beast, which struggled with all its might. We then requested the Regent to apply his right eye, shutting his left, to the glass at the top of the machine.

"Tsong-Kaba!" exclaimed the Regent. "The louse is as big as a rat!" After looking at it for a moment, he raised his head and hid his face with both hands, saying the creature was horrible to look at.

The Regent tried to dissuade the others from examining it; but his influence failed to make any impression. Every one, in turn, looked through the microscope, and started back with cries of horror. The lama secretary, seeing that his little animal scarcely moved, advanced a claim in its favor. We removed the nippers and let the louse fall into the hands of its owner. But, alas! the poor victim did not move. The Regent said laughingly to his secretary: "I think your louse is unwell. Go and see if you can get it to take some medicine; otherwise it will not recover."

No one wished to see other living creatures, so we continued the entertainment by passing a small collection of microscopic pictures before the eyes of the spectators. Every one was charmed, and exclaimed with admiration, "What prodigious ability the French have!"

The Regent told us: "Your railways and your aerial ships no longer astonish me so much. Men who can invent such a machine as that are capable of anything."

The First *Kalon* was so delighted with the productions of our country that he took a fancy to study the French language. One evening we brought him, in accordance with his wish, a French alphabet, each letter of which had the pronunciation written beneath it in Tibetan characters. He ran his eye over it, and then, when we proposed to give him some explanations, he replied that they were not necessary, as what we had written was quite clear.

The next day, as soon as we appeared in his presence, he asked us what was the name of our Emperor.

"Our Emperor is called Louis Philippe."

"Louis Philippe! Louis Philippe! Very well!" He then took his style and began to write. An instant afterwards he gave us a piece of paper on which was written, in very well formed characters, LOUY FILIPE.

35
Politics and Customs

D URING the brief period of our prosperity at Lhasa, we had also tolerably intimate communication with the Chinese Ambassador, Ki-Chan. He sent for us twice or thrice, to talk politics, or, as the Chinese phrase it, to speak idle words. We were much surprised to find him so intimately acquainted with the affairs of Europe. He spoke a good deal about the English and Queen Victoria. "It appears," said he, "that this woman has great abilities; but her husband, in my opinion, plays a very ridiculous part. She does not let him meddle with anything. She laid out for him a magnificent garden full of fruit trees and flowers of all sorts, and there he is always shut up, passing his time walking about. They say that in Europe there are other countries where women rule. Is it so? Are their husbands also shut up in gardens? Have you in the kingdom of France any such usage?"

"No. In France the women are in the gardens, and the men in the state."

"That is right; otherwise all is disorder."

Our frequent conferences with the Chinese Ambassador, the Regent, and the Kashmirian governor, contributed not a little to secure for us the confidence and consideration of the inhabitants of Lhasa. On seeing the number of those who came to visit us, and to be instructed in our holy religion, augment from day to day, we felt our hopes enlarge and our courage increase. Yet, amidst these consolations, one thought constantly vexed us: it was that we could not present to the Tibetans the inspiring spectacle of the majestic and touching festivals of Catholicism. We were convinced that the beauty of our ceremonies would have a powerful influence over the minds of these people, so eager for all that appertains to external worship.

The Tibetans, as we have already observed, are eminently religious; but, with the exception of a few contemplative lamas who withdraw to the summits of mountains and pass their lives in the hollows of rocks, they are very little disposed to mysticism. Instead of confining their devotion within their inner hearts, they like, on the contrary, to display it by outward acts; and accordingly pilgrimages, noisy ceremonies in the lamaseries, prostrations on the tops of their houses, are practices extremely to their taste. The Tibetans usually have in their hands the Buddhist rosary, turning and twisting it, and incessantly murmur prayers, even when they are engaged in business.

There exists at Lhasa a very touching custom, and we felt a sort of jealousy at finding it among infidels. In the evening, just as the day is verging on its decline, all Tibetans stop business and meet together—men, women and children, according to their sex and age—in the principal parts of the town and in the public squares. As soon as groups are formed, every one kneels down, and they begin slowly and in undertones to chant prayers. The religious concerts produced by these numerous assemblages create throughout the town an immense solemn harmony, which operates forcibly on the soul. The first time we witnessed this spectacle, we could not help drawing a painful comparison between this pagan town, where all prayed together, and the cities of Europe, where people would blush to make the sign of the cross in public.

The prayer which the Tibetans chant in these evening assemblies varies according to the seasons of the year; on the contrary, that which they repeat on their rosary is always the same and consists of only six syllables—*Om mani padme houm.* This formula, which the Buddhists call, by abbreviation, the *Mani*, is not only in every one's mouth; it may be seen written everywhere in the streets, in the squares, and in houses. On all the flags that float above the doors or from the summit of the public edifices, there is always a *Mani* printed in Landza, Tartar, and Tibetan characters. Certain rich and zealous Buddhists maintain, at their own expense, companies of lama sculptors, whose business it is to diffuse the *Mani.* These singular missionaries travel, chisel and mallet in hand, over hill, dale, and desert, engraving the sacred formula upon the stones and rocks.

According to the opinion of the celebrated Orientalist, Klaproth, "*Om mani padme houm*" is merely the Tibetan transcription of a Sanskrit formula brought from India to Tibet. Towards the middle of the seventh century of our era, the famous Hindu, Tonmi-Sambhodha, introduced writing into Tibet; but as the Landza alphabet, which he had at first adopted, seemed to King Srong-Bdzan-Gombo too complex and too difficult to learn, that monarch invited the Hindu scholar to draw up an easier writing, better adapted to the Tibetan tongue. Accordingly, Tonmi-Sambhodha shut himself up for a while and composed the Tibetan writing now in use, which is merely a modification of Sanskrit characters. He also initiated the monarch into the mysteries of Buddhism, and communicated to him the sacred formula, "*Om mani padme houm,*" which spread rapidly through all the territory of Tibet and Mongolia.

In Sanskrit this formula has a distinct and complete meaning, which cannot be traced in the Tibetan idiom. Among the Hindus, *Om* is the mystic name of the Divinity, with which all their prayers begin. It is composed of A, the name of Vishnu; of O, that of Siva; and M, that of Brahma. This mystic syllable is also equivalent to the interjection Oh and expresses a profound religious conviction: it is, as it were, a formula of the act of faith. *Mani* signifies a gem,

a precious thing; *padma* is the lotus, and *padme* is the voca-
tive of the same word; *houm* is a particle expressing a wish,
a desire, and is equivalent to our *Amen*. The literal sense,
then, of this phrase is this:

Om mani padme houm.

Oh, the gem in the lotus! Amen.

The Buddhists of Tibet and Mongolia have not been content with this clear and precise meaning, and have tortured
their imaginations in their endeavors to find a mystic inter-
pretation of each of the six syllables composing the sentence. They have written an infinity of voluminous books,
wherein they have piled one extravagance on another, to
explain their famous *Mani*. We may, however, observe, as
it appears to us, that it bears some analogy to the literal
meaning: "Oh, the gem in the lotus! Amen." The gem
being the emblem of perfection, and the lotus of Buddha,
it may be considered that these words express the desire to
acquire perfection in order to be united with Buddha, to be
absorbed in the universal soul. The symbolic formula, "Oh,
the gem in the lotus! Amen," might then be paraphrased
thus: "Oh, may I obtain perfection, and be absorbed in
Buddha! Amen."

36

Beginning of Trouble

WE were scarcely a month in Lhasa before the numerous inhabitants of this town grew accustomed to speaking with respect and admiration of the holy doctrine of Christ. The peace and tranquillity we enjoyed, the distinguished protection which the Tibetan Government extended to us, the sympathy with which the people seemed to surround us, all inspired us with the hope that, by the aid of God, we might lay in the very capital of Buddhism the foundation of a mission, the influence of which would soon extend itself among the nomad tribes of Mongolia. The moment seemed to have come when the Tartar pilgrims might at length learn, at Lhasa, the only doctrine which can save the souls of men and civilize nations.

Such were the plans we were forming for the establishment of a mission at Lhasa; but at this very moment the enemy to all good was hard at work to ruin our projects, and to remove us from a country which he seems to have chosen for the seat of his empire. Having heard here and there evil words of ill omen, we realized that the Chinese Ambassador was secretly plotting our expulsion from Tibet. The vague rumor of this persecution had, in fact, nothing about it to surprise us. From the outset we had foreseen that, if difficulties assailed us, they would emanate from the Chinese mandarins. Ki-Chan, in fact, could not bear to see the Tibetan government receive with so much favor a religion and some strangers, whom the absurd prejudices of China had so long driven from her frontiers. Christianity and the French name excited too forcibly the sympathy of the people of Lhasa not to arouse Chinese jealousy. An agent of the court of Peking could not, without anger, reflect on the popularity which strangers enjoyed in Tibet, and on the influence which they might one day exercise in a country which China had every interest in keeping under her dominion.

It was determined, therefore, that the preachers of the religion of the Lord of Heaven should be driven from Lhasa. One day the Ambassador, Ki-Chan, sent for us, and, after sundry attempts at cajolery, ended by saying that Tibet was too cold, too poor a country for us, and that we would better think of returning to France. Ki-Chan addressed these words to us with a sort of indifferent, careless manner, as though he supposed there could be no sort of objection to them. We asked him if, in speaking thus, he proposed to advise or to command. "Both the one and the other," he replied coldly.

"Since it is so, we have first to thank you for the interest which you seem to have in our welfare, in telling us that this country is cold and miserable. But you must know that men such as we do not regard the comfort and conveniences of this world; were it not so, we should have remained in our own kingdom of France. For know, there is not anywhere a country comparable with our own. As for the imperative portion of your words, this is our answer: 'Admitted into Tibet, by the local authority, we recognize no right in you, or in any other person, to disturb our abode here.'"

"What? You who are foreigners presume still to remain here?"

"Yes, we are foreigners, but we know that the laws of Tibet are not like those of China. The Pebung, the Kashmirians, the Mongols, are foreigners like us, and yet they are permitted to live here in peace; no one disturbs them.

206 HIGH ROAD IN TARTARY

What, then, is the meaning of this arbitrary proceeding of yours, in ordering Frenchmen from a country open to all people? If foreigners are to quit Lhasa, why do you stay here? Does not your title of *Kin-Tchai* (Ambassador) distinctly announce that you yourself are but a foreigner here?"

At these words, Ki-Chan bounced on his velvet cushion. "I a foreigner!" cried he. "A foreigner! I, who bear the authority of the great Emperor; I, who only a few months since, condemned and exiled the *Nomekhan!*" (He was referring to the trial and banishment of the King of Tibet, who had been found unworthy of his high position.)

"We are acquainted with that affair," we replied. "There is this difference between the *Nomekhan* and us, that the *Nomekhan* came from Kansu, a province of the Chinese Empire, and we come from France, where your great Emperor is nobody; and that the *Nomekhan* assassinated three Grand Lamas, while we have done no injury to any man. Have we any other aim than to make known to men the true God, and to teach them the way to save their souls?"

"Yes, as I have already said to you, I believe you to be honest people; but then, the religion you preach has been declared wicked and is prohibited by our great Emperor."

"To these words, we can only reply this: The religion of the Lord of Heaven does not need the sanction of your Emperor to make it a holy religion, any more than we, its missioners, need that sanction to come and preach our religion in Tibet." The Chinese Ambassador did not think it expedient to continue this discussion; he dryly dismissed us, declaring that we might rest assured he would make us quit Tibet.

We hastened to the Regent, in order to acquaint him with the melancholy interview we had had with Ki-Chan. The First *Kalon* had been made aware of the projects of persecution which the Chinese mandarins were hatching against us. He endeavored to reassure us, and told us that, protecting in the country thousands of foreigners, he was powerful enough to give us the protection which the Tibetan Government extended to all. "Besides," added he, "even if our laws did prohibit foreigners from entering our country, those laws could not affect you. Religious persons, men of prayer, belonging to all countries, are foreigners nowhere; such is the doctrine taught by our holy books. It is written: 'The yellow coat has no country; the lama no family.' Lhasa being the peculiar assembling place and abode of men of prayer, that title of itself should always secure for you liberty and protection."

This opinion of the Buddhists, which constitutes a religious man a cosmopolite, is not merely a mystic idea written in books: we have found it recognized in the manners and customs of the lamaseries. When a man has his head shaved and assumes the religious habit, he renounces his former name to take a new one. If you ask a lama of what country he is, he replies, "I have no country, but I pass my time in a lamasery." This manner of thinking and acting is accepted even in China, amongst the bonzes and other classes of religionists, who are called by the generic name of Tchou-Kia-Jin—a man who has left his family.

Respecting us, there developed a controversy of several days' duration, between the Tibetan Government and the Chinese Ambassador. Ki-Chan, in order to insure better success to his aim, assumed the character of defender of the Grand Lama. This was his argument:

As he had been sent to Lhasa by his Emperor to protect the Living Buddha, it was his duty to remove from the latter whatever calculated to injure him. Certain preachers of the religion of the Lord of Heaven, animated, no doubt, by excellent intentions, were propagating a doctrine which, in the end, tended to destroy the authority and power of the Grand Lama. Their avowed purpose was to substitute their religious belief for Buddhism, and to convert all the inhabitants of Tibet, of every age, condition, and sex. What

would become of the Grand Lama when he had no wor-
shipers? Does not the introduction into the country of the
religion of the Lord of Heaven lead directly to the destruction of the sanctuary of the Potala, and consequently to
the downfall of the Lamaistic hierarchy and the Tibetan
Government?

"I," said he, "who am here to protect the Grand Lama,
can I permit at Lhasa men who propagate such formidable
doctrines? When these doctrines shall have taken root, and
it will be no longer possible to extirpate them, who will be
responsible for such a misfortune? What shall I reply to the
great Emperor, when he shall reproach me with my negli-
gence and cowardice? You Tibetans," said he to the Regent, "you do not comprehend the gravity of this matter.
Because these men are virtuous and irreproachable, you
think they are harmless—but that is a mistake. If they remain long at Lhasa, they will hypnotize you. Among you,
there is not a man capable of disputing with them upon
religion. You will not be able to keep from adopting their
belief, and then the Grand Lama will be undone."

The Regent did not share these apprehensions, with
which the Chinese Ambassador endeavored to inspire him.
He maintained that our presence at Lhasa could not in any
way be prejudicial to the Tibetan Government. "If the doctrine which these men hold," said he, "is a false doctrine,
the Tibetans will not embrace it. If, on the contrary, it is
true, what have we to fear? How can the truth be prejudicial to men? These two lamas of the kingdom of France,"
he added, "have not done any harm; they are animated
with the best intentions towards us. Can we, without good
cause, deprive them of the liberty and protection which we
extend here to all strangers, and particularly to men of
prayer? Can we make ourselves guilty of an actual and certain injustice, through an imaginary fear of some possible
evil to come?"

Ki-Chan reproached the Regent with neglecting the inter-

ests of the Grand Lama; and the Regent on his part accused
Ki-Chan of taking advantage of the minority of the sovereign to tyrannize over the Tibetan Government. For our
part, in this unfortunate contest, we refused to acknowledge
the authority of the Chinese mandarins, and declared that
we would not quit the country without a formal order from
the Regent—who assured us that they should never extort
from him any such thing. The quarrel became more and
more bitter every day. Ki-Chan resolved to take on himself
to expel us from the country. Matters reached such a crisis
that prudence obliged us to yield to circumstances, and to
oppose no further resistance, for fear of compromising the
Regent and of becoming, perhaps, the cause of lamentable
dissensions between China and Tibet.

By further opposing this unjust persecution, we might
irritate too vehemently the Chinese, and furnish pretexts
for their project of usurping the Tibetan Government. If,
on our account, a rupture should unhappily break out between Lhasa and Peking, we should inevitably be held responsible for it; we should become odious in the eyes of the
Tibetans, and the introduction of Christianity into these
countries would encounter thereafter greater difficulties
than ever. We, therefore, considered that it would be better
to submit, and to accept with resignation the rôle of the
persecuted. Our conduct should prove to the Tibetans that
at least we had come among them with peaceful intentions,
and that we did not intend to establish ourselves there by
violence.

After having maturely considered these points, we proceeded to the Regent. On learning that we had determined
to leave Lhasa, he seemed sad and embarrassed. He told us
he greatly wished he had it in his power to secure for us a
free and tranquil abode in Tibet; but that alone, without
the support of his sovereign, he had found himself too weak
to resist the tyranny of the Chinese who, for several years
past, taking advantage of the infancy of the Grand Lama,

had assumed unprecedented claims in the country. We thanked the Regent for his good will; then we went to call upon the Chinese Ambassador. We told Ki-Chan that, being far distant from all protection, we had resolved to leave Lhasa, since he was determined to compel us to do so; but that we protested against this violation of our rights.

"Well, well," answered Ki-Chan, "you cannot do better! You must depart; it will be better for you, better for the Tibetans, better for me, better for everybody." He then told us that he had ordered all preparations to be made for our departure; that the mandarin and escort who were to accompany us had been selected. It had been even arranged that we should depart in eight days, and that they should take us along the route which leads to the frontiers of China.

37

Farewell, Lhasa

THE evening before our departure, one of the secretaries of the Regent entered our lodging and presented to us, in his name, two great ingots of silver. This attention on the part of the First *Kalon* affected us deeply, but we considered we ought not to accept this sum. That same evening, on going to his palace to bid him adieu, we took back to him he two ingots. We laid them before him on a small table, protesting to him that this proceeding resulted from no ill feeling on our part; that, on the contrary, we should always remember with gratitude the good treatment we had received from the Tibetan Government, during the short stay we had made at Lhasa; that we had no hesitation in expressing our belief that, if all had depended on the Regent, we should have continued to enjoy in Tibet the most tranquil and honorable abode; but that, as to this money, we could not receive it without compromising our conscience as missioners.

The Regent did not seem in any degree irritated by this proceeding. He told us that he understood our conduct, and could appreciate the objection we had expressed; that he would not insist on our accepting this money, but that still he would be very glad to make us some present upon separating. Then pointing to a dictionary in four languages, which he had often observed us turning over with interest, he asked if this work would be agreeable to us. We thought we might receive this present without compromising in any way

211

the dignity of our character. On our own part, we expressed
to the Regent how happy we should be if he would deign
to accept, as a reminder of France, the microscope which
had so excited his curiosity. Our offer was kindly received.

At the moment of parting, the Regent rose and addressed
to us these words: "You are going away, but who can know
future events? You are men of astonishing courage. Since
you have been able to get thus far, I know that you have in
your hearts a great and holy resolve. I think you will never
forget it. For my part, I shall always bear it in mind. You
understand me: circumstances will not permit me to say
more."

"We understand," we replied to the Regent, "the full
meaning of your words, and we will implore our God to
realize one day the purpose they express." We then parted,
our hearts bursting with grief, from this man who had been
so kind to us, and by whose means we had formed the hope
of making known, with God's help, the truths of Christianity to these poor people of Tibet.

When we re-entered our house, we found the Kashmirian
governor awaiting us. He had brought some provisions for
our journey: some excellent dried fruits from Ladak, some
cakes made of flour, some butter and eggs. He insisted upon
spending the evening with us, assisting us in packing our
trunks. As he intended shortly to visit Calcutta, we charged
him to give news of us to the first Frenchman he should
meet in the English possessions in India. We also gave him
a letter, which we entreated him to get forwarded to the
representative of the French Government in Calcutta. In
this letter we briefly explained the circumstances of our
stay in the capital of Tibet, and the reasons for our departure. It seemed to us advisable to take this measure,
when we were about to commence a journey of a thousand
leagues, along frightful roads continually bordered with
precipices. We thought that, if it should be the will of
God for us to be buried amid the mountains of Tibet, our

friends in France would at least know what had become of us.

The same evening, Samdadchiemba came to bid us adieu. On the day that the Chinese Ambassador had resolved to make us leave Tibet, our dear neophyte had been taken from us. It is needless to say how hard and painful this trial was, but to this measure neither the Regent nor ourselves could offer any objection. Samdadchiemba was a native of the Province of Kansu, directly subject to the Chinese authority. Although our influence with Ki-Chan was not very great, we did persuade him to promise that Samdad-chiemba should suffer no injurious treatment, and should be sent back safely to his family. Ki-Chan promised this, and we have since ascertained that he was true to his word.

The Regent was full of kindness towards our neophyte. As soon as he was separated from us, the Regent took care that he should want for nothing; he even gave him a sum of money to provide for his journey. With what circumstances allowed us to add to this, Samdadchiemba was enabled to amass a small fortune, and to place himself in a position to return in a fitting manner to his paternal dwelling. We advised him to go to his aged mother and fulfill the duties which filial affection dictates, to instruct her in the mysteries of the Christian Faith, and to cause her to enjoy at her last moments the benefit of baptism; then, when he should have closed her eyes, to return and pass his days among the Christians.

To say the truth, Samdadchiemba was not an amiable young man. Sour, savage, and sometimes saucy, he was by no means an agreeable fellow traveler; yet he had in him a groundwork of honesty and devotion, quite capable, in our opinion, of compensating for the perversities of his nature. We felt at parting from him a deep affliction, and all the more so because we had never suspected the existence, at the bottom of our hearts, of so strong an attachment to this young man. But we had made with him a long and painful journey; we had endured together so many privations and so much misery that, unconsciously, our existence was, so to speak, fused with his. The law of affinity which unites men to each other acts with much more power amidst suffering than in prosperity.

On the day appointed for our departure, two Chinese soldiers came, early in the morning, to inform us that his Excellency Ly, peace envoy among kingdoms, awaited us at breakfast. This personage was the mandarin whom the Ambassador Ki-Chan had appointed to accompany us to China. We accepted his invitation; and, as the departure was to take place from his house, we had our luggage transported thither.

We proceeded to the house of the mandarin, where eighteen horses, already saddled, were awaiting us in the courtyard. The three best were standing apart, reserved for the mandarin Ly and ourselves. The fifteen others were for the soldiers, and each was to take the one which fell to him by lot.

Before we mounted, a strong-limbed Tibetan woman, very fairly dressed, presented herself; she was the wife of Ly. He had been married to her six years, and was about to leave her forever. They had had only one child, which had died in its infancy. As these two were never again to see each other, it was but natural that at the moment of separation there should be a few words of adieu. The thing was publicly done, and in the following manner:

"We are going to part," said the husband. "Do you stay here and sit quietly in your room."

"Go in peace," replied his wife. "Go hence in peace, and take care of the swellings in your legs." She then put her hand before her eyes, as if to make us believe she was crying.

"Look here," said the peace envoy, turning to us, "they are odd people, these Tibetan women. I leave her a well-built house, and plenty of furniture almost new, and yet she is going to cry! Is she not content?"

After this adieu, so full of unction and tenderness, every one mounted, and the party set out down the streets of Lhasa.

When we were out of the town, we perceived a large group awaiting us. They were those inhabitants of Lhasa with whom we had had more intimate acquaintance during our stay in that town. Many of them had begun to learn the truths of Christianity and seemed to us sincerely disposed to embrace our holy religion. They had assembled on our road to salute us and say a final farewell. Amongst them was the young physician, still wearing on his breast the cross we had given him. We dismounted and addressed to these Christian hearts a few words of consolation: we exhorted them courageously to renounce the superstitious worship of Buddha, to adore the God of the Christians, and ever to have full trust in His infinite mercy. Oh, how cruel was that moment, when we were obliged to part from these well-beloved catechumens, to whom we had as yet only pointed out the path of eternal salvation.

At length, after an hour's march, we reached the banks of the river Bo-Tchu. We found there a Tibetan escort, which the Regent had ordered to conduct us to the frontiers of China. It was composed of seven men and a lama, the latter holding the office of district governor. With the Chinese escort, we formed a caravan of twenty-six horsemen, not including the drivers of a large herd of yaks that carried our baggage. We cast a long last look at the city of Lhasa, still visible in the distance, and said in the depths of our hearts, "God's will be done!"

The return journey was a long and arduous one. At length we arrived, safe and sound, at the frontiers of China, where the climate of Tibet gave us a very cold farewell. In crossing the last mountain, we were almost buried in the snow which fell thick and fast, and which accompanied us into the valley. There, at the Chinese town, Tatsienlu, the snow changed to pelting rain. It was the early part of June, 1846, and three months since we had departed from Lhasa. According to the Chinese count, we had traveled 5,050 li, or about 1,680 miles.

The Tibetan escort had accompanied us faithfully during the journey. Now, at this town, after two days' rest, they left us, to return to Tibet. We sent back with them a letter to the Regent, in which we thanked him for having assigned us so devoted an escort, who had throughout kept us constantly reminded of the good treatment we had received at Lhasa. On parting from these good Tibetans, we could not help shedding tears, for insensibly, and as it were without our knowledge, ties had been formed which it was painful to sever. The lama governor secretly told us that he had been charged to remind us, at the moment of separation, of the promise we had made to the Regent. He asked if they might count on seeing us again at Lhasa. We replied that they might, for at that time we fully intended to return some day to Tibet. But God's ways are not our ways. We never saw Lhasa again.

Index

Red Banner, 20, 39
Regent. *See* Tibet
River of the Lord, 130
Robbers, 5, 136–139
Rope making, 106–107
Russian trade, 14

S

Salt, 120; lake, 62; mines, 62
Samdadchiemba, 2, 169, 187, 213
Sandara, 77, 85, 96
Season of land vapors, 105
Seven lakes, 1
Shabartai, 24, 34
Sheep, 67, 71
Shih-Tsui-Tzu, 76
Shugan, 125, 127
Spies, 161
Srong-Bdzan-Gombo, King, 202
Strawberries, 104
Sulphur springs, 144

T

Tangar, 109
Tangla, hot springs of, 143; mountains, 140
Tansan, 110
Taolai-yin-gol, 119
Tartar, camel, 33, 63; education, 29; feast, 73; food, 29; horsemanship, 30; hospitality, 21, 26; hotel, 47; sheep, 29; tea, 19; trade, 34; veterinary science, 75; wine, 22

Tartary, eagle of, 43; landscape, 20
Tatsieniu, 215
Tchanak-Kampo, 138
Thieves, 150
Three Lakes, 23
Tibet, French art in, 182; King of, 206; Regent of, 163, 194
Tibetan, cold, 125–127, 131–133; Embassy, 112; hospitality, 188, houses, 155, 156; prayers, 37, 201; wife, farewell of, 214; writing, 202
Tonmi-Sambhodha, 202
Tortuous River, 130
Trade, 15
Tree of Ten Thousand Images, 77, 82, 83–84
Tsaidam, 120
Tsamba, 109
Tsong-Koba, 77
Twin Ravines, 11

V

Vapors, poisonous, 123
Venison, 39, 104

W

Women, 200

Y

Yak, 98
Yang-pa-erh, 5
Yellow River. *See* Hwang-Ho
Yüeh Ping, Festival of, 25

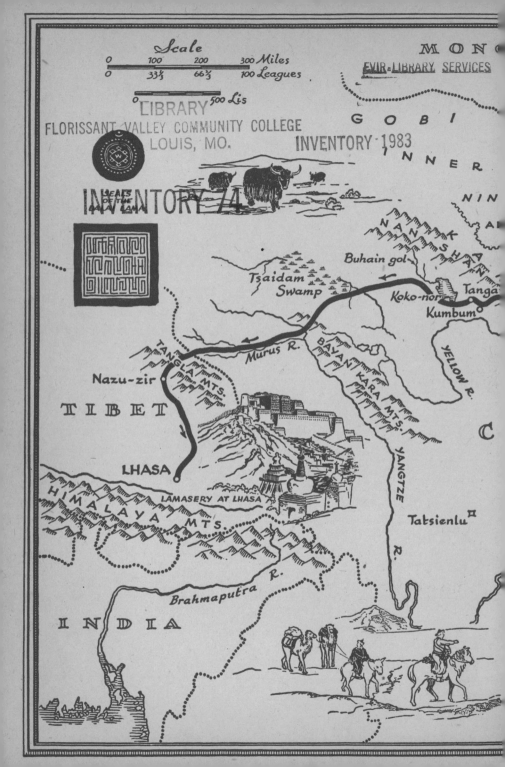

Scale

| 0 | 100 | 200 | 300 Miles |
| 0 | 33⅓ | 66⅔ | 100 Leagues |

0   500 Lis

MON

EVIR-LIBRARY SERVICES

G O B I

I N N E R

NIN

AI

K

N A N S H A N

Buhain gol

Tsaidam
Swamp

Koko-nor

Tanga

Kumbum

YELLOW R.

Murus R.

BAYAN KARA MTS.

TANGLA MTS.

Nazu-zir

T I B E T

C

LHASA

YANGTZE R.

H I M A L A Y A
M T S.

LAMASERY AT LHASA

Tatsienlu

Brahmaputra R.

I N D I A